Animal Intuition

Communicating with Pets, Animal Spirits, and the Energies of the Natural World

Thea Strom

STERLING ETHOS
New York

STERLING ETHOS
New York

An Imprint of Sterling Publishing Co., Inc.

ISBN 978-1-4549-4674-8 (hardcover)
ISBN 978-1-4549-4675-5 (e-book)

For information about custom editions, special sales, and premium purchases,
please contact specialsales@unionsquareandco.com.

Printed in Malaysia

2 4 6 8 10 9 7 5 3 1

unionsquareandco.com

Cover design by Melissa Farris
Interior design by Christine Heun
Cover and interior illustrations by Chervelle Fryer

For Embla and Elias

Contents

Introduction: My Story

When I was twelve years old, I traveled from my home in Norway to visit my dad in Florida for a few months, where he lived with a woman named Lady C. Lady C was an animal communicator who went on boats to swim with wild dolphins and whales. She was a healer. She was a psychic and a medium. Her house was filled with exotic rescued animals and two wolf dogs. It was like one big magical party, and my soul was drawn to all of it.

I dove headfirst into books on meditation and divination. Lady C's friend Frannie, also a medium, came to stay while I was there. Frannie gave me a book she had written about her experience communicating with a little boy who had drowned. She also provided me with two of her guided meditation cassettes that involved connecting with angels.

When I went back to Norway, I continued to steep myself in the world of spirituality for years, though becoming a medium or animal communicator was never a goal I had set specifically, nor did I think it was something I could actually do myself. I just knew that I had to move in this direction: The pull was too strong.

The metaphysical remained a strong interest for me throughout my teens. However, I remained ignorant of just how sensitive I was to energy. When I was younger, I knew that I could sense how a person was really feeling, but I didn't think much about it. It wasn't a constant gift, nor did I think it was very powerful in me. But, much later on, I realized that I was wrong that whole time. I think we are all much more psychic and sensitive than we think. We often just have a hard time identifying how our abilities really work.

In my case, I was quite the empath without realizing it. An empath is what we call someone who feels other people's energy and emotions as if these were their own. A person might do this entirely subconsciously. For example, you might walk into a room and begin to feel irritated and short-tempered for no reason, without knowing that another person in the room is seriously irritated at their boss over something. Or, as you start talking to a coworker, you notice an ache in your lower back that wasn't there before, without realizing that your coworker has severe back issues. We are unaware that we're doing it, so we assume it's our own because it feels exactly like our own. I think of it as our intuitive bodies picking up on anything unusual or out of balance in our surroundings in order to warn us about it (just in case it's something to worry about).

One thing that I loved to do in my teens was go to the annual metaphysical fair in Oslo, Norway, where I lived. I listened to all the lectures and perused the crystal and tarot deck booths. At one of these fairs, I decided to take the leap and join a free one-hour workshop on mediumship. After a brief lecture, the workshop presenter paired all of us up to do a short exercise. He asked us to close our eyes and take a moment to mentally call on our partner's deceased loved ones to connect with us. My partner, a middle-aged woman who was a complete stranger, sat across from me. I closed my eyes, and immediately I felt this whoosh of energy going through my body as if I were being lifted or stretched upward. Then, in my mind's eye, I saw the fuzzy outline of a man. He was like a bear, big and tall, with dark hair. When I mentally asked him for more information about who he was to my partner, he proceeded to give me the most mind-blowing feeling of love for this woman. The feeling was so overwhelming that I felt high on it. I shared everything I was sensing with my partner, and she, in turn, through tears, told me that I was describing her deceased husband. Before the workshop ended, I felt this incredible urge to hug her, not for me, and not for her, but for him.

This was my first time doing mediumship intentionally. The rest of the day, I felt as if I were walking on air. I felt like I was on track. I was nineteen years old, but I knew that mediumship or doing readings would play a big part in my life in some way. Whenever someone asks me when I first realized that I could connect to spirits or animals or energy, that moment at the metaphysical fair is one I think back to. However, it was only when I combined the realization of my empathic qualities with concerted training in mediumship that I truly became the animal communicator that I am today.

In my early twenties I moved to the United States with my now-husband, and that's when I started to make genuine efforts to meditate every day. Although it was more for self-care than enlightenment, this is when I began to have some odd, unsolicited experiences with mediumship. On two separate occasions, random spirits connected to me, out of the blue. These experiences felt different than those at the workshop I had taken previously, in that they were utterly unexpected and, honestly, quite uncomfortable, like an intrusion in my personal space. It was enough for me to think that maybe I should sign up for a mediumship class to see if I could learn to control this ability a bit more. So that's what I did.

I took several classes in mediumship, learning to connect to the spirit world, to connect to people's passed human loved ones. One day, early on in my development as a medium, I was out running errands, and I had to drive by our house between one errand and another. As I drove by our driveway, I suddenly saw an image in my mind's eye of our cats' food bowl completely empty and I heard the words *I'm hungry*. It was so unexpected and odd, because I knew our cats' food bowl had been full before I left. It seemed impossible that our two cats could have finished it, since I'd left just a couple of hours earlier. I decided to swing by home quickly just to double-check, in case this wasn't just my brain imagining things. I got home and discovered the cats' food bowl was empty, and our new kitten Gilly sitting expectantly next to it, with a very round, full tummy. Gilly had apparently finished the whole bowl, and decided she wanted more. My husband and I, having only had grazers in our past, were not aware that some cats would continue to eat as long as there was food available. Gilly taught us that lesson pretty quickly after that.

When I had the opportunity to try to intentionally communicate with a living animal through one of my mediumship mentors, I jumped at the chance. I wanted to see if this was an ability I could hone and use for other people, and not just as a way for my cat to demand more food from me. I was supposed to connect to a dog, to see what he wanted to share about his life and how he was feeling in his body. I remember connecting to him, and, in my mind's eye, I was immediately brought down to his front leg, to the bone. Turns out he had bone cancer in that leg, and his humans were trying to figure out what to do in terms of treatment. Communicating with the dog felt so natural to me, and so easy in comparison to the other types of readings I had done before. It was such an eye-opening experience that I fell in love with animal communication immediately. I had always loved animals. I had had several special connections with pets previously, but never a proper conversation like this. So I reached out to some friends, and asked if I could practice animal communication with their pets, and I have never stopped since.

Animal communication and mediumship have been an amazing way for me to more deeply experience the world, and I hope that you are able to take the first steps toward practicing it for yourself. While you may not be able to achieve mastery from this book, I hope that it will help you sharpen your intuition and maybe practice a few exercises with your companion animals, animal spirit guides, or the souls of animals who have passed on. To live in this world is to be surrounded by the energies of others, and I hope this will add another dimension of understanding to your everyday life. Good luck, and if you find that this practice speaks to you, I encourage you to seek out more classes and mentorships so you can take it to the next level.

✦

PART ONE

All Creatures Great and Small

CHAPTER 1

The Basics of Animal Communication

E ven if I hadn't had any profound conversations with animals growing up, I did always feel very connected to them. I was ten years old when my dad secretly got us a kitten while my mom was on vacation. We named her Klara, and she was the love of my life. At first, Klara was wild, like most kittens (she would literally climb our walls), but she quickly developed into an affectionate and connected companion.

Klara would put me to bed every night, and during the day, she joined me on all my adventures at home. We had a large area of tall grass that reached my waist, where Klara and I would play Marco Polo. I would hide in the grass and meow for Klara to find me. Once she did, she would run to go hide and meow until I found her. She was my closest companion growing up, especially in my teens when I was going through difficult times.

I moved away from home eventually, and Klara had to stay with my mom because my new apartment didn't allow cats. One time when I went back home to visit, Klara had been missing for two weeks. I immediately went out and called for her—not just verbally, but I called out to her soul. She came back home that very day. The connection we had was always an unforced, natural one. I would think about her, and she would come running. I didn't think of it as communication between us, necessarily, but as a very close intuitive bond. She understood me, and I understood her. I didn't question it, nor did I feel the need to label it.

I think this is how many of us think about our connection with our companion animals. We understand them on an unspoken level, and they understand us. Animal communication is essentially built on that same connection. Animal communication is when we bring that subtle communication that is already happening to a conscious level.

When I introduce myself to new people and they hear that I am an animal communicator, I think some of them imagine that I am like Dr. Dolittle. That when I walk down the street, I can hear all the animals in the neighborhood talking out loud to themselves or to each other. Or that when I walk into a room, all the animals rush toward me and tell me about their problems. Or that just because I can talk to animals, they automatically do what I ask them to. I wish I had that kind of superpower: to make anyone, including animals, do what I want! Animal communication is actually a lot more subtle, and a lot more about listening and fostering mutual respect. It's also a lot more about creating understanding and working together to find solutions, instead of controlling an animal's behavior. Additionally, while many humans may talk to themselves out loud (myself included), in my experience animals do not walk around broadcasting their thoughts for no reason. Animals are naturally much more present in the moment, existing without worrying so much about the past or the future.

What Is Animal Communication?

All animals use several "languages" to communicate with other animals and humans—vocal language (your typical meows, barks, neighs), body language, and telepathic (intuitive/psychic) language—and they will often use all of these at the same time. Telepathy is really just the ability to communicate across a distance, through the mind and through energy. Telepathy can happen because *we are all connected*: The seeming distance or boundaries between us simply do not exist, or rather, they are irrelevant to our connection. You may have heard the quote by French theologian and philosopher Pierre Teilhard de Chardin: "We are not human beings having a spiritual experience. We are spiritual beings having a human experience." His quote sums it up well. We are all spiritual beings incarnated in our present physical bodies in order to experience life. We are not our bodies. We are, at our essence, still spiritual beings, and our souls are not limited in the way our physical bodies are. Things like physical distance do not matter to our souls. Our souls are energy capable of connecting to anything anywhere, with the right intention and focus.

Animals are spiritual beings, too (souls within bodies), and thus we can connect with them not only on a physical level, but also on an energetic or spiritual level, soul to soul and heart to heart. In fact, the ability to communicate with animals is something we are all born with: because we all have a soul, we are all spirit. It is our natural state of being to be able to connect with other souls. Just like other animals, humans naturally communicate through vocal language, body language, and telepathically (often without realizing it). This is how we are wired. But because all these types of communication function like muscles, if we don't use them, they may atrophy. In modern Western society, telepathic communication is typically just never encouraged. Most of the time it is actually ridiculed and taught to be a figment of our imagination. Therefore, the telepathic "muscles" have atrophied for many people. Luckily, like all muscles, we can practice using these abilities until they become as useful as our other modes of communication.

When I say *telepathy*, most people think that means that I hear an animal talk to me in full sentences in my head. That's not quite how it works. *Telepathy* can be a misleading word, which is why I prefer to use the term *animal communication*. The animal's communication is actually coming through to me in a variety of impressions. The animal is not sending me words to communicate. They are sending the energy of what they are trying to communicate, and then that is translated into impressions in my body and mind. We say that the communication is translated through our "*psychic senses*." You may have heard of these before. We have six major psychic senses:

Clairvoyance: "clear sight"

Perceiving energy through our internal sense of sight. Information might come through as pictures, symbols, or movie-like clips in our mind's eye. It might feel similar to daydreaming.

Clairaudience: "clear hearing"

Perceiving energy through our internal sense of hearing. We often experience this as if it's coming through from our own brain, similar to when you replay a conversation in your mind. Clairaudience can come through as words, sounds, songs, or whole sentences.

Clairsentience: "clear feeling"

Perceiving energy through our internal sense of feeling, both physical sensations and emotional feelings. You might perceive a dog's hip pain as a pain in your own hip, or you might perceive a cat's sadness as a welling up of sadness within yourself.

Claircognizance: "clear knowing"

Suddenly knowing information without knowing how we know it.

Clairgustance: "clear taste"

Perceiving information through our internal sense of taste. We might suddenly taste peanut butter because the animal wants to talk about their favorite human treat. This will likely be subtle. If you imagine the taste of peanut butter in your mouth, it will be similar to what you perceive through your clairgustance.

Clairalience: "clear smell"

Perceiving information through our internal sense of smell. We might suddenly smell cow manure, because maybe the animal lives on a farm with cows. This also will be subtle, experienced in a similar way as if you were going to imagine a smell in your mind.

✦

You might notice that one or two of the psychic senses are more prominent for you than the others. This is usually in accordance with how active your corresponding physical senses are. For example, if you are a very visual person, maybe if you paint or do other visual work, you might have a strong *psychic* sense of sight as well. The same goes for the other senses. However, don't get too hung up on, or attached to, which is your strongest sense right now. First of all, you might be wrong. You might have a preconceived idea of which sense is your strongest that isn't actually accurate. Maybe a psychic once told you that you're very clairvoyant, and you start to ignore your stronger sense of clairsentience. Information gets easily lost in translation that way if we over-identify with one sense, and don't trust our other senses. Secondly, it's possible you could change dominant senses in the future. Ideally, we would like to become well-rounded with our psychic senses, so that information can come through strongly in all of them. This helps the communication to come through as easily, clearly, and accurately as possible.

Try bringing to mind an image of a tree. Notice if the image is crystal clear to you, or if it is hazy. Notice if the image is sturdy and deliberate in your mind, or if it is just a brief flash. You might think this is an exercise in being able to tell if you have a strong sense of psychic sight. I actually have a very different point to make: Information coming through your psychic sense of sight might appear in any of these ways, and that is normal. It might come through as hazy, or clear, or as a sturdy image, or as more of a brief flash. Clairvoyance doesn't come through crystal clear every time. When I receive information through my clairvoyance, most of the time the images are just brief flashes, or I only see vague outlines.

Often, I am shown just enough for me to get the gist of what the animal wants to tell me. This can also change, even in the span of a single reading, as some things come through clearly while others are more hazy. The same goes for all the psychic senses. If you bring to mind a smell, you might experience a similar variation in clarity. This is important to know, because many people will discount information coming through their psychic senses if the impressions aren't crystal clear. I do readings professionally many times a week, and have done so for years, and still most of the time the impressions coming through from an animal are hazy, and in brief flashes, not fully fleshed-out scenes that stay put in my head. The impressions might be subtle, and varied, and that is totally okay.

I want to note that some people have what's called aphantasia, and are not able to bring to mind or experience visual imagery. Some people have the same but with their auditory sense, or with any of the other senses. Some people have hyperphantasia, which means they are able to visualize something vividly, as if they were seeing it with their physical eyes. The same can happen with the other senses. Most people might be somewhere in between. There is no need to panic if you have aphantasia, with visual imagery or other senses. Everyone's brain functions a little differently. If your mind's eye is blank when you try to visualize, then try bringing to mind the same thing but through a different sense.

Oftentimes, information from an animal will come through several of our senses at once. This can be helpful, because it helps us interpret correctly what the animal is trying to communicate. For example, if you connect to your cat and receive an image of their kibble in your mind's eye, and you get a feeling in your body of enthusiasm, and you also feel a pain in your stomach, that could tell you that your cat loves the kibble they get, but they also get a tummy ache from it. That could explain the diarrhea they've been having. Or if you are connecting to your dog, and you hear the words *play-date* in your mind, you see an image of other dogs in your head, and you also feel anxiety in your body, that could be your dog's way of sharing that they feel anxious in social situations with other dogs.

Here's a fun fact: As you start to develop your own abilities as an animal communicator, you might find that you improve in other types of intuitive readings without any additional effort. This is because everything that goes under the heading of "psychic abilities" is interconnected. This includes animal communication, plain psychic readings, remote viewing, medical intuition, intuitive card readings, psychometry, angel readings, mediumship, spirit guide readings, scrying, etc. *Psychic abilities* just refer to the ability to receive previously unknown information through one's psychic senses. The main differences between the different types of readings is in who or what you are connecting to, and the topics you're talking about. The process, however, is very similar between them. So if you work on one type of reading, you are using and strengthening your psychic senses, and, as a result, you will have an easier time doing another type of reading. Your psychic senses are like muscles in the body. You might begin to take boxing lessons once a week and thus strengthen your muscles that way. If you then begin to take rowing classes, you will automatically have an advantage, because you have already begun to condition the muscles in your arms. The same goes for doing different types of readings.

The following exercise is one you can do to strengthen those same mental pathways that are at work when you receive information through your psychic senses. This exercise helps you learn to focus on your internal senses, and it helps you strengthen each individual sense.

Internal-Senses Exercise

Find a quiet time to sit down, close your eyes, and practice bringing to mind (or "imagine," if you will) different sensory impressions. Feel free to make your own list of impressions to call up.

✦ The sound of waves crashing on the beach. The sound of a church bell ringing. The sound of a cat meowing. The sound of a dog barking.

✦ The taste of spicy Indian food. The taste of peanut butter. The taste of chocolate chip cookies. The taste of coffee.

✦ The feeling of excitement over getting to meet your favorite person. The feeling of seeing a friend you haven't seen in a long time. The feeling of sadness over losing something or someone. The feeling of amusement over a good joke.

✦ The sensation of someone stroking your forearm. The sensation of touching a dog's fur. The sensation of a cat lying on your legs. The feeling of a great hug.

✦ The image of sunlight shining through the autumn leaves. The image of a sunset. The image of a dog wading in water. The image of a cat waiting for their dinner.

Some of these sensations are likely going to feel very subtle and hard to bring to mind. If there is a sense that you just aren't able to imagine anything with, that is okay. As I mentioned previously, it could be that you have aphantasia with that particular sense. Please note that this is different from having a sense that you *can* imagine things with, but it's just very little or very subtle. If that's the case, then I encourage you to continue to work with that sense, to strengthen it more. You can even devote a whole practice session to focusing on imagining impressions only through that particular sense.

Connecting

When we connect with animals, we are connecting soul to soul with them, or heart to heart. We become aware of their communication with us through a shift in our perception, from experiencing communication through our physical senses, to experiencing communication through our souls and psychic senses. This shift happens as a result of relaxing the logical thinking mind and moving into a receptive brain state. Some might call this a light trance, which is essentially the same state we are in when we daydream. When we are daydreaming however, our focus wanders. When we are communicating with an animal, we are in the same open state of mind, but our focus is on the animal and on the internal impressions we receive from them, instead of on the outer world around us.

Most of the time, the communication that the animal is sending to us is quite subtle. This means that we need to practice quieting the actively thinking logical brain, in order to notice what is coming through from the animal. We learn to do this through practices like meditation. Meditation is super helpful for learning to clear the clutter from our mind, and to strengthen our ability to focus. However, it is important to note that when we engage in animal communication, we are usually not in a deep meditative state. This can be confusing, because meditative practices are such an important part of learning how to be present so that we can "hear" the animal, but in the actual conversation with an animal we are in a heightened state of awareness. It's an almost hypersensitive state, while also having a center of stillness and focus that has been developed by the meditation practice. Communication with an animal does not happen in the same slow state of mind we are in during deep meditation. Successful animal communication may often feel as if we were raising our energy and lifting our spirits, opening up to the exciting world of an animal, while being grounded and calm at our center.

Now, don't get scared off by the idea of having to commit to a meditation practice! Meditation can just be a time you set aside to bring your focus to the present moment. You could do a mindfulness meditation by focusing on your breath for five minutes. Or you could listen to guided meditations (I have one available in the resources section at the end of the book). Or you could do movement meditation, like qi gong, gardening, or even a walk in nature, which can help you clear your mind and get present and centered. In fact, spending time with your animal companions can be a meditative practice when it's done mindfully. Your meditation practice does not need to be perfect and you don't need to be a master at it in order to develop your animal communication skills. I'm honestly not the best meditator, but I do it before almost every session. It prepares my mind to connect, and it helps me maintain the muscles of focus and quiet my own thoughts to become aware of what the animals want to share with me.

Mindfulness Exercise with Animals

Take some time today to relax with your animal companion. Your goal here is to stay present with them physically and mentally. If your mind wanders, gently bring your awareness back to your animal companion. Notice the way their chest expands every time they take a breath. Feel how yours expands, too. Notice your animal's movements, the way they move their body. If you start thinking of your to-do list or about work, bring your awareness back to your body, back to your breath. Notice the animal's breath, and be present with them.

If you don't have any living animal companions, take some time outside in nature, bringing your awareness to your breath and your body. Become present with the wildlife around by, for example, listening to the sound of squirrels scurrying up trees, or birds singing. Notice the breeze, and notice your own breathing along with it. Watch the way the animals are fully focused on their task, or how immersed they are in their rest. Any time you notice your mind wandering, bring your awareness back to your body, back to your breath, and back to the movement of nature around you. In this exercise we are just practicing focusing on the present, releasing the constant chatter in our mind as a result, and practicing becoming aware of what is.

Focused Awareness

After clearing the clutter from your mind and getting into a state of receptivity, the next step in animal communication is to expand your awareness and direct it to the animal. You know how you are able to keep your eyes on one thing in the room, while keeping your awareness on something different happening at the other end of the room, without looking over there? Maybe you've done that before when eavesdropping on a conversation happening next to you while looking in the opposite direction. That's kind of similar to what we're doing with our awareness when connecting to an animal. Physically we might be sitting in front of the animal's human (if we're connecting to someone else's animal companion), and we might even be looking at the person, but energetically we are stretching our awareness to the animal we are connecting with, listening in to what they have to say.

The animal could be in the same room as you, or in a different room, or even on the other side of the world. Remember when I said your soul is limitless? It could even potentially connect to an animal on the other side of the world and receive clear communication from them. Remember, it's not like we're communicating through vocal language with them. We're communicating through energy, soul to soul, and the energy of our souls is boundless. (Even though I think it's sweet when clients put me on speakerphone with their animals, it's not actually necessary for the animals to even hear my voice.)

Our awareness is on what we are connecting with, and it should stay there throughout the session. What your awareness is on is what determines which energy you intuitively tune into or communicate with. If you were wanting to intuitively tune into a friend's energy, you would place your awareness on your friend. If you wanted to intuitively tune into the energy of a home you're thinking of purchasing, you would place your awareness on that home. If you wanted to connect and communicate with a passed loved one, you would place your awareness on that loved one. If you want to connect and communicate with an animal intuitively, you would have to place your awareness on that animal.

When expanding and directing your awareness to an animal, all it takes is having a clear intention to expand your awareness, and a clear intention for where you want to direct it. Some people like to use visualization to help them expand and direct their awareness. In animal communication we can do this by visualizing a bright light at the center of our own chests, at what we might call our heart-centers. And then we can visualize that light expanding out to become a beam of light that connects to the animal's heart-center. If you can't visualize that clearly, that's OK. Like I said, all you need is a clear intention to expand your awareness to the animal, and think about the animal you want to connect with. If the animal is your own animal companion, you already have a heart-to-heart connection anyway. If the animal is not your own animal companion, then you might like to have a picture of them in front of you, to help you direct your awareness to that particular animal and keep your focus on them.

The following exercise gives you some experience with expanding and directing your awareness and energy in a conscious way to whatever you want to connect with. The more you can practice expanding and directing your awareness, the clearer and stronger your connection will be with animals. This exercise is heavily focused on visualization. It's okay if you can't visualize it clearly. Just try to imagine it in whatever way you can, and let it be what it is. What's most important about this exercise is that you are expanding, directing, and focusing your awareness. There are no right or wrong answers or experiences with this exercise. Just relax, try it out, and see what happens.

Exercise:
Expanding Your Awareness

Take a moment to close your eyes and visualize a light shining at the center of your being, perhaps at your solar plexus or in the center of your chest. This light is part of your energy. With each exhale, see or feel that light shine brighter and grow bigger and bigger, until it fills your entire body. Then with your next exhale, visualize or feel it expand out beyond your body, into the space around you, growing bigger around you, so you are completely surrounded by your energy. Now sense what your energy feels like when it is expanded out around you like that. Feel for where the edges of your energy are. What does that space outside of your own energy feel like, compared to yours? (You might not have words to describe it, or you might not feel anything very strongly, and that's okay.)

Now visualize stretching and directing your energy down into the chair or whatever surface you are sitting on. You are merging your energy and awareness with the chair, experiencing what it feels like to be this chair. What do you notice? Do any feelings or sensations come up for you? What textures or quality of material do you notice? What emotions? Do any images pop up in your mind's eye? Give yourself a moment to just experience what comes through without judging it, keeping your awareness and energy in the chair.

Visualize disconnecting from the chair, and stretching your energy further out, directing it to a nearby tree outside. Focus your awareness on this tree, merging your energy with it. Again, pay attention to what you're sensing. Do any feelings or sensations arise? What textures do you notice in the tree? Do any emotions come up here? Or do any images pop up? What perspective do you get on your surroundings from here?

Now visualize disconnecting from the tree, and stretch your energy, directing it to a wall of a nearby building, and again take note of what impressions you get as you merge your awareness with this wall. Do any feelings or sensations come up? What textures or materials do you notice here? What emotions do you feel? How about images in your mind's eye? Take a moment to just feel yourself merged with this wall, and notice anything and everything, no matter if it makes sense or not.

Visualize yourself disconnecting from that wall, and call all of your own awareness and energy back to your body, easily bringing it back from all those places you visited. Notice how your body feels. Observe the room around you, and the feeling of your breath, and open your eyes and stretch.

Love and Permission

Animal communication is a language of love. We connect through love, respect, and recognition that we are all one. When connecting to an animal for a reading, we do this heart to heart. Therefore, before you begin connecting, it is always helpful to first bring your awareness within to your own heart and to your feelings of love for all of creation, particularly for animals. Steep yourself in that feeling of love. Then direct your awareness to the animal you want to connect with and visualize a bright light emanating from your heart center. If you can't visualize it, that's all right. Just know that as you focus on your heart center, your energy there will naturally expand. Expand this light in your heart, and send it out to the animal, connecting this light with the animal's heart.

If you are not in the same room as the animal, it might feel easier to imagine expanding out your heart energy to connect to their heart if you have a picture of the animal in front of you. Once you have connected heart to heart, send all that loving energy you generated in yourself to the animal. Now you have created a strong connection, and you can mentally introduce yourself and ask the animal if they would be open to communicating with you. Asking the animal's permission to communicate is an important step of respect and courtesy. A yes from an animal can feel like a subtle opening up or agreement from them. It's not always hearing the word yes in our mind. A no can feel like being shut out or pushed away. However, it is very rare that you would ever get a no from the animal in response. I have found that most animals are happy for the opportunity to talk to their human companions, directly or through an animal communicator.

Communicating: How to Send Messages Effectively to an Animal

Directing your thoughts to an animal is enough to send the energy of what you wish to communicate. Speaking out loud to an animal can also work, because as you're talking out loud, you are sending the energy of what you wish to communicate. But you do not need to speak out loud for them to understand you. Directing your thoughts silently to them works just as well. That energy is then translated for the animal so they can understand it.

The same thing happens the other way. They send the energy of what they wish to communicate. That energy is then translated into internal impressions (through our psychic senses), so that we can interpret and understand it.

While thinking thoughts to the animal is generally enough to communicate, it can be helpful to clarify our messages by also bringing to mind the images, feelings, and additional sounds of what we wish to communicate. For example, if you wish to communicate to an animal that you would love for them to get along with another animal in the house, you would say that to them mentally with words, and also bring to mind an image of the two animals hanging out together in the same space completely relaxed, and also bring to mind the feeling of how peaceful the house would be, and how happy the humans in the house would be. All these sensory impressions help clarify exactly what you mean and wish to communicate to the animal.

It's important to note that, when communicating with an animal about behavioral challenges, you want to focus on the thing you want the animal to do, instead of the thing you want them to stop doing. For example, if you want the cat to stop scratching the furniture, it would be counterproductive to say, "Don't scratch the couch," because you are sending the cat the energy and image of them scratching the couch. At best, you're sending mixed signals, and at worst you're encouraging the animal to do the thing you don't want them to do. A much clearer way to communicate, would be to say, "Scratch only the scratching posts, please. The couch is for resting on." That way you are sending clearer communication, redirecting the animal to what you would love them to do instead. Of course it helps to ask the animal why it does the undesired behavior and if there's anything that can help change it. We'll go deeper into this sort of thing later on in the book.

How We Receive

We receive the communication from the animal by keeping our awareness on them (as we did in the earlier exercise, when we practiced focusing our awareness). This is our way of "listening" while noticing anything and everything coming through our psychic senses: images in our mind's eye, words or sounds in our head, feelings in our body, etc.

Thanking and Disconnecting

When we are done with the conversation, it is important to practice good manners and thank the animal for connecting and sharing. If you are just starting out, it would be kind and considerate to thank the animal for helping you improve your animal communication abilities as well.

Once you are ready to disconnect, you don't need any ritual for breaking the connection. The most important thing is where you place your awareness. Once you start to think about other things in your day, that's going to break the connection naturally. If you feel that it's helpful to have something concrete to do to signal the end of the session, you might want to do a visualization, of seeing the light connecting your heart with the animal's heart, and then visualizing that light dissolving or falling away. You could also do something symbolic, like washing your hands after a session, as a concrete signal to yourself that you have broken the connection.

Overview: The Process of Animal Communication

1 Get centered and present, clearing your mind.

2 Bring to mind feelings of love, expand your heart energy, and direct that energy to connect to the animal's heart. You can use a picture of the animal to direct your energy to if you are not in the same room as the animal.

3 Direct your thoughts to the animal: Send love to the animal, introduce yourself, and ask for permission to communicate.

4 Keep your awareness on the animal throughout the session as a way of listening to the animal and directing your communication to them.

5 Notice all subtle impressions coming through your psychic senses.

6 Thank the animal and disconnect.

The Conversation

While I do often find myself relaying messages from an animal to their human about wanting more treats, and which types of treats they prefer, that is not all that will come up in a session. So what kinds of information normally come through in a reading with an animal?

✦ Their personality

✦ How are they are feeling emotionally

✦ Their physical appearance (including any prominent physical traits that aren't apparent)

✦ Their mannerisms

✦ Their family relations (their thoughts about any other animals they live with, human family members, whoever they're most bonded with, etc.)

✦ Their habits (good or bad)

✦ Any behavioral challenges

✦ Their health, physical wellness, how they are feeling in their body

✦ Their diet and how they feel about it

✦ Their interests, likes/dislikes, any favorite toys/activities/
foods, anything they would like more of or less of

✦ Their thoughts on their home environment

✦ Their daily schedule—if they like it or if it can be improved
in some way(s)

✦ Their past before they came to their current humans

✦ What they consider to be their job or responsibility; their
greater role in this life and in their human's life

✦ Messages for their humans

This list is really intended to give you an idea of what kinds of things an animal might bring up, or what kinds of things might be helpful for their human to know. Personally, when doing a proper animal communication session for someone else, I am a fan of allowing their animal to lead the conversation as much as possible in the beginning of the reading. I do this for a couple of reasons. First of all, it respects the animal as an equal participant in the conversation, and they get a chance to voice the things that are important to them, instead of it being all about the human's needs and questions. Second, it gives the animal communicator a chance to bring through verifiable evidence that they are indeed connecting to the animal.

This list is especially relevant when it comes to communicating with other people's animal companions. If you are communicating with your own animals, you likely already know what their personality is like, and what their favorite things are. They probably won't find it necessary to tell you that they have a kink in their tail. But if you're connecting to someone else's animal, those things do become relevant, because it becomes part of the verifiable evidence of your communication with the animal.

Verifiable evidence is essentially information that the animal tells you about themselves or about their life, which can prompt their human to say, "Yes, that is absolutely right." Verifiable evidence is important in a reading, first, to give *you* a clear sense that you are in fact connecting to the animal. When you have that evidence, you'll know definitively that what you're receiving is not just your brain making things up. Second, verifiable evidence can give the *animal's human* a clear sense that you are connecting to their animal. They are much more likely to take to heart the messages that can't be verified, like an "I love you" or detailed guidance, if you've also brought through information that shows you are connecting. If I don't bring through all the detailed evidence first, then the human might discount the whole reading and it would all have been for naught.

In addition, we need some kind of system to make sure that we're connecting properly, for ethical reasons, because animal communication is an intuitive art, not a science. If we're going to be speaking on behalf of another being, especially if that being is living, we need to make sure we have a reliable connection.

Verifiable evidence is generally easier to bring through at the beginning of a session, before the human has told you anything about the animal and before they've told you what questions they have for the animal. Basically, I like to start off my readings without knowing anything about the animal beforehand other than name and type of animal, and I will just ask the animal to tell me about themselves or just ask them to talk about what's been going on for them or whatever they feel is most important to bring up for their human.

I might be having a day where I'm just feeling off, tired, sick, or the animal isn't willing to communicate for whatever reason. These can all affect the reading. If, during a session I get information that just isn't resonating with their human and is clearly wrong, or nothing is coming through, I can take that as a good sign to reschedule. Should I be having a bad day or just a day with low energy, using this system of bringing through verifiable evidence stops me from giving erroneous information and causing harm to the animal.

Another reason bringing through evidence is important is that it helps us to be 100 percent percent certain of which animal we're connecting to. I will sometimes have clients who have a large number of animals. For example, let's say my client has five dogs and they make an appointment for me to talk to only one of the animals, who happens to be the least outgoing of the pack. There's a big chance that one of the other dogs will take over the conversation if that's part of their personality, particularly if the outgoing pet thinks this is their only chance to talk to its owner. Even if I intended to connect with the first dog, it might be one of the others who jumps in instead. Details and evidence help clarify who it is you're connecting to.

I do want to note also that a few pieces of information being off in animal communication is totally normal and expected, either due to misinterpretation or their human not remembering certain details. However, if an overwhelming amount of information is off and you know you're not connecting in the right way, that might tell you that either you're connecting to a different animal than you intended or, for whatever reason, the connection just isn't working out.

Now you might be thinking, "But I just want to communicate with my own animals. How can I bring through verifiable information that I don't already know?" Verifiable evidence isn't as important when communicating with your own animals. Doing readings with your own animals is, however, a topic that comes with its own challenges, deserving of its very own section, so we will dive into that later on in the book.

Your Brain as a Filter

A question I get a lot from animal communication students is this: "How do you discern between what's just from your imagination and what is from the animal?" This question is somewhat misleading, because your imagination is not the devil. It is not out to disrupt your readings. You want to become friends with your imagination, because it is just a tool—a tool for your brain to create things and a tool through which energy can describe itself. So in a reading with an animal, the information coming through is being described through your imagination.

Your brain is essentially a box of all the experiences and knowledge that you've gained through your life. It's filled with all the animals you've known, it's filled with all the people you've known, all the knowledge you've gained, all the experiences you've had. The energy of what the animal wishes to communicate is being filtered through this box, so this box is part of the vocabulary you have to work with when "translating" the energy of what the animal is communicating with you. Let's say the cat you are connecting to is telling you that she is very skittish and deals a lot with anxiety. That might come through for you as an image of your old cat who was very skittish and anxious. It's a shorthand way for the energy to explain itself, by showing itself to you in that one image of a cat you already know. It doesn't mean that this cat is your old cat. But you're seeing your old cat because of the similarities, and it's easier for your brain to translate the energy that way.

Different animal communicators have different "boxes of vocabulary," since we all have different experiences and mental references. This means that each animal communicator can connect to the same animal and still end up with slightly different readings. If we have two animal communicators connect to the same animal, the readings should generally be in the ballpark of each other, but one person might be better at picking up on the medical aspects from an animal, while another person might be better at picking up on the emotional things going on for the animal.

How I think of it is that the animal is sending a lot of information at the same time about one particular subject, and not all that information makes it through the animal communicator's brain or translation, partly because it's a lot of information at one time, partly because the animal communicator might not have all the right "vocabulary" (references in the brain) to describe it all, and partly because we all have different interests and specialties in what we like to pick up on and communicate. For example, let's say a dog is sending information on how he loves to go with his owner to the owner's cabin by the lake, and he gets super excited to go, but he also tends to get motion sickness in the car on the way there, since the road going up to the cabin has lots of twists and turns. One animal communicator might pick up on the trip up to the cabin and how excited the dog is about it and focus in on what the cabin looks like and that there's a lake and a park nearby, but the motion sickness is just a very brief mention. Another animal communicator might pick up on the trip to the cabin and how excited the dog gets about it and focus in on the fact that they get motion sickness in the car on the way there, and what might help it, but might not get any details about what the cabin looks like. So it is completely natural for your own readings to differ somewhat from other people's readings with the same animals, because we all have different perspectives, as well as different strengths and interests.

Since the animal's communication is being filtered through your own personal history and experience, as well as through your own unique imagination, some surprising references might come up as metaphors in the reading. For example, lately I have been diving back into the Harry Potter movies. Since it's a current interest of mine, it's sometimes easier for my brain to translate energy into Harry Potter references during readings. For example, if the animal wants to share their personality with me, I might see an image of the character Luna Lovegood as shorthand for an animal that is perhaps a bit ditsy and out of touch on the surface, but is actually very in tune with what's going on around them at heart. It's not that the animal has seen Harry Potter (necessarily), but they're sharing the information about themselves through energy that is then translated by my brain into those references for me to be able to understand. Years ago I went through a brief period where I would see an image of different hats on the animals' heads to signify their personality: a top hat for the perfect gentleman, or a broad-brimmed fancy sun hat for a gal who liked to have a lot of fancy fun. Admittedly, it took me a few readings to understand that the hats were metaphorical, not literal (which ultimately enabled me to stop asking a lot of awkward questions like "Um . . . does your dog happen to have a top hat?").

Because of the way in which information is processed through our brain, this also means you have to actively keep a very open mind in order to allow what the animal truly wishes to communicate to reach your consciousness. Your prejudices, thoughts, and ideas will all create a filter through which you will interpret the information you receive. If you are, for example, very anti-euthanasia, you might subconsciously block a message from the animal that they might want to cross over in that way. If you think it's impossible to train a cat, you might subconsciously block a message from a cat identifying themselves as being highly trainable.

The best way to approach a session is with an open mind. Allow yourself to be surprised. There is just as much variety of life experience and unique opinions among animals as there is among humans. Going into a session with the attitude that you already know what the answer is blocks true communication. Keep your mind open, even about things you are pretty sure you know about already, and allow the animals to show you what's true for them.

Communication Styles

All animals are different in how they like to communicate. You could say they all have different communication styles. Their communication style is completely individual to each animal, and not based on the type of animal they are or their breed. Just as with humans and their different level of skill in how well they communicate with other humans, animals each have different levels of skill in communicating as well. Some are great communicators; others are less adept at communication. Some will want to talk about everything all at once and be thrilled to connect, while others might be much slower, and not that interested in sharing. Some will boldly state their behavioral challenges ("I peed on the bed yesterday. So what?"), while others might beat around the bush a little bit and be really embarrassed about it ("Yesterday I did something in the living room that I shouldn't have, but I am not sure I want to talk about it"). Some will want to go into great detail about their life, and some will be much more vague about it.

In general, it does seem that animals who tend to be very vocal or communicative in other ways with their human also tend to be great communicators telepathically (or at least very talkative telepathically), but that's not a hard-and-fast rule. Some very calm and quiet animals might surprise you when you communicate with them. Intelligence levels *may* play a part in how skilled an animal is at communicating, but that's one of those things that is hard to quantify. Intelligence can mean a lot of things—it's not just an animal's ability to do a trick, nor even the ability to communicate well. Intelligence may be a more nuanced quality that might escape even an animal's owner.

Why is it Easier to Communicate with Some Animals Than with Others?

Just as you might feel that you click better with certain humans than with others, the same will happen between you and certain animals. Some you will feel a much more immediate kinship with than you do with others, so naturally the conversation will flow more easily, too.

If there are certain types of animals you know a lot about and have lots of experience with personally, that may mean you will more readily recognize the types of information coming through when you communicate with them. If you connect to a type of animal you don't have much experience with, it's most likely going to take longer to recognize the energy that they're sharing with you, because you aren't as familiar with it. Let's say you're connecting to a goat, and you don't know what activities are normal for goats, or even what they typically eat. As a result, you're likely to get bogged down by doubting the information coming through, and you might not even recognize some of it.

Does the Type of Animal Determine How Easy They are to Communicate with?

Personally, I have not found that to be true. Rather, it seems to be very much based on the individual, and does not have anything to do with what type of animal it is. I have communicated with a whole range of animals: dogs, cats, guinea pigs, rabbits, small birds, chickens, fish, lizards, snakes, horses, goats, and even wild animals, like skunks, big cats, and whales. I have had just as wonderfully deep and pinpoint-accurate readings with certain chickens as I have had with dogs that compete in agility competitions. The success and depth of a reading is always going to depend on the individual animal and their own skills and personality. It's important not to make assumptions about an individual animal before we've tried connecting with them.

I personally have not received any direct communication from insects, but I don't think that necessarily means anything. I believe all of nature can be connected with and communicated with in its own way, even if it isn't the same as connecting to bigger animals.

Do Animals Lie?

In the type of animal communication I teach in this book, you have a direct telepathic connection with the animal, and in a lot of ways it's very much like interacting with a human in a conversation. When you hang out with a friend over coffee to catch up on each other's lives, your friend will make decisions on what's most important for them to talk about, and how they're going to present the topics to you, as well as what things to leave out of the conversation. They might exaggerate certain things, and downplay other things. The same goes for our furry, feathered, and scaled friends.

In my experience, animals don't lie, per se. However, they might present something to me from their own perspective that others might disagree with, or that might not fully match up with the reality of the situation (on the other hand, they might have a much better understanding of the reality of the situation than others). The animal might also choose not to mention something, or they might skirt around the bigger issue at hand. They might also choose to paint a situation as rosier than it really is.

That's the wonderful and also somewhat frustrating part of animal communication: We are dependent on the way the animal wants to share their life. I find it helpful to have the animal's unique take on something, even if it isn't the exact truth of the situation, because that gives me information on how I should approach them if I am going to talk them through some of the issues at hand. If, for example, a cat doesn't feel that it's a big deal that they constantly bully the other cats away from their human, then that shows me it might be helpful to explain to the cat why it is a big deal for the others. Or if a dog skirts around the issue that they've pooped inside the house for the past month, that might tell me that they're actually embarrassed about it, and it might be important for me to show lots of compassion and understanding to them. That way the dog and their human can work on shifting the behavior together.

If an animal is holding something back, or if they are presenting something a little differently than the reality of the situation, I might pick up on that in their energy, in a psychic manner, but sometimes I am fooled, too. If I am connecting with an animal I feel is holding back information, it's part of my job to help them feel comfortable enough to share more with me in order to help them in the best way possible. That doesn't always happen, though, and as an introvert myself, I think it's understandable that some animals will have a hard time sharing with complete strangers. We all have different communication styles, and we work with what we have to foster understanding between us all.

Your Own Animal Companions

You might be reading this book only to be able to connect to your own animal companions. Does it work the same as a professional reading when you communicate with your own pets? How do you verify that you're actually connecting to them, and that it's not just your own brain making things up?

Connecting to your own animal companions works the same way as when connecting to others'. When you are talking to your own animals, whether out loud or in your mind, you are automatically sending them the energy of what you're trying to communicate. They generally will get the gist of what you're trying to say, a lot of the time. We humans also tend to walk around broadcasting our thoughts without realizing it. So even things you are not intending to communicate to your animal—things you only thought about, things you never said out loud—your animal is likely picking up on many of those things. This is something we just naturally do, and this is also why it's hard to keep secrets from our animals.

You will want to be mindful of what you communicate to your animal companions. That also means taking the time not only to tell them with words, but to try to imagine through your senses what it is you're trying to communicate. When your animal companion is sending *you* what they wish to communicate, those impressions coming through your senses are likely going to be quite subtle. It often feels like the impressions coming through are arising from within you, which is what makes this process tricky, because it feels like your own brain making things up, even if the message is actually from the animal. These impressions tend to feel even more subtle when they're from our own animal companions, because that energy already feels so familiar to us. We have spent so much time with our own animal companions that it can be hard to tell where our energy ends and their energy begins.

As opposed to connecting to other people's animals, when you're con-necting to your own, you don't have the opportunity to bring through verifiable evidence, because you likely know most things about them already. Therefore, it's natural for the logical brain to get involved and question if what came through is really from the animal, or just something you knew or suspected already. Because of that, there's often more noise from your brain that you have to set aside while you connect.

Another challenge is that we have an emotional tie to the outcome of a conversation with our own animal companions. Let's say your cat is peeing outside the litter box, and your vet couldn't say why, so naturally you want to ask your cat why they're doing this. Since you love your cat deeply, and you don't want them suffer, you are already emotionally invested in this question or, more importantly, in the answer of it. Our fears about potential answers will automatically cause us to get in the way of our own connec-tions with our animals, making it hard to truly hear what their answers may be. Additionally, it's very easy for us to take our animal's behaviors person-ally, and those personal feelings can cloud our connection.

When we are afraid of what the answers are, we will often rush through our communication with our animals. We might not take time to sit down with them and open up fully, because of our fear. When we are tied to the outcome of a conversation, we might be extra afraid that we will misinterpret what's coming through, and make the situation worse. Especially if it's health related, we're afraid we will misinterpret or miss something important. So, as you can see, there are many more layers to work through when connecting to our own animals than there are when connecting to an animal with whom we don't have an emotional, personal bond.

However, in a lot of ways, the personal bond you have with your own animals is also what makes it much easier to connect to them than to someone else's animal companions. You have already built up an emotional bond with your own. A heart-to-heart connection already exists there, and starting a communication can be as simple as placing your awareness on the animal. Additionally, your animal companions likely will feel more motivated to communicate with you directly, and have themselves be understood more fully by you, because of your bond. Some animals can be quite worried around strangers, and will communicate much more readily with people they feel close to.

Since you probably know your animal companions so well already, there's less opportunity to bring through information that can act as evidence that you are truly connecting. So the evidence comes in a different form: through the shift in their behavior, through their responsiveness to you, and through the shift in your relationship. This means you're going to have to have a little bit more faith as you try connecting, and have patience as you see your connection to your animal deepen over time. You will likely see them becoming more responsive to your suggestions, but, most importantly, your bond will deepen as well. Animal communication is a journey that improves your connection over time.

There are two ways you could go about connecting to your own animal companions:

1 Having a direct conversation with them (the method I have laid out earlier in this book).

2 Having a delayed conversation with them. This is where you sit down to ask your animal questions, and let them surprise you with their responses later on.

For method 1, you would approach it using the techniques I've taught you already. Just remember: For most people, connecting to your own animals is going to require a lot more quieting of the logical thinking brain. The information coming through is probably going to feel a bit more subtle than it does with others' animals. It will require you to open your mind and relax the thinking brain, and just allow in the responses from your animal. It also will require you to be much more mindful of a few things:

✦ Become mindful of your own fears. If you notice them coming up when you're trying to connect, gently place those fears to the side, and direct your focus back to your animal.

✦ Notice if you feel yourself rushing your communication with them. That is usually a sign that you are subconsciously trying to force the animal's responses in anticipation of a certain answer, or it could mean that you are afraid of the answer. Can you dedicate a good chunk of time to just sitting and communicating with your animal without a goal or a particular answer in mind?

✦ Notice if there is tension in your body when you're connecting. That may be a sign that you are subconsciously trying to force the animal's responses to produce a certain answer. Can you release that tension? Can you really settle in and become present with your beloved animal companion? Can you focus your love on them, and allow their replies to come through for you?

If you feel stuck between trying to distinguish between what feels like your own thoughts and what is from the animal, set a time limit for the exercise of connecting. You might say "Okay, for the next fifteen minutes, I am just going to acknowledge and accept anything and everything that comes through from my animal companion." After you're done connecting and once those fifteen minutes are up, you're free to engage the logical brain again and see how things make sense to you. But if you start trying to distinguish between your thoughts and those of the animal in the middle of your connection, you're likely not in the open, intuitive, receptive state we want to be in during animal communication.

So when you sit down to communicate, become mindful of your own fears, become mindful of when you might be trying to rush things, and become mindful of where you are tensing and pushing your mind and body to get to a certain answer. Then continue to adjust yourself, continue to release those fears, and continue to take your focus back to your animal, allowing their answers to come to you.

Some of you might still feel that an active conversation with your own animal in this way can be difficult. In that case, you can try method 2, in which you receive communication from your animal more passively, at a later time. What you do is this: Connect as you normally would, then ask your animal your questions, letting them know that you don't need the answers right now, but would appreciate it if they could communicate the answers to you at any time within the next day or so. Then just go about your day, and your animal companion will likely try to answer your questions when you're least expecting it.

With this method, it's up to you to become mindful of the thoughts and other impressions that pop up for you throughout the day, especially when you're engaging in more mindless tasks like doing the dishes, driving, showering, cleaning the floor, anything where you naturally disconnect mentally from what your body is doing. It's usually during those moments that the impressions will come through more clearly from your animal. If it's from the animal, you're likely going to feel that the communication came out of the blue. If it's from your brain, the message will likely be a logical, linear thought like "The answer must be X, because A, B, and C."

Maybe you are doing the dishes and letting your mind wander to how excited you are about going out to dinner tonight. Then, all of a sudden, you see an image in your mind of your dog, and you hear the words "My back hurts." We can identify that as being from your dog, and not your brain, because it wasn't part of any linear, logical thinking in the moment. There was no connection between the thought about going out to dinner and your dog having back pain. The other way you can identify a thought from your animal is if the thought repeats itself throughout the day. So if it comes out of the blue, especially while you are doing mindless tasks, and if you notice the same thing coming up more than once, those might be good signs that the message is from your animal companion.

What if You Have Multiple Animals?

If you have multiple animals, how can you know for sure that you are connected to the right one? Just as in sessions with other people's animals, you can ask your own animal companion to tell you about themselves in a way that helps identify who they are, so you're sure of who you're talking to. You already know them, so they are just giving you information to help you be sure of who you're connected to. If they show you that they're the one who loves to attack the toilet paper, you'll know that you're connecting to the one who has an unhealthy obsession with the toilet paper in your house.

With our own animals, the validation of our communication often comes in the form of a deepening of your bond over time, as well as shifts in behaviors. However, many people are still going to feel the need for validation that is clear-cut and immediate. Even if your intention is only to ever use animal communication with your own pets, I encourage you to practice with other people's animals, so you can get a good sense of what it feels like when you are actually connecting, and to build your confidence in your abilities. If you have friends around you who might be open to this, try connecting to their animals, and ask for feedback from your friends about what came through from the animal. If you've been successful with other people's pets, you can trust that the same methods will work with your own, even if you don't have the immediate validation.

Exercise: Connecting to Your Own Animals

✦ Set aside fifteen minutes or so to connect to your animal companion. Decide that during fifteen minutes, you will just accept and acknowledge everything that comes through.

✦ It might be helpful to first take a moment to write out some of the main worries you have about what could come up in your conversation. Acknowledge that those are just anxieties and are not necessarily the truth of the situation. Decide to put those worries to the side for now, so that you can be open to what your animal companion truly wants to share with you.

✦ Get clear on some of the topics you're hoping your animal companion will want to talk about. Maybe write a list of questions you have for them.

✦ Take a moment to meditate or just focus on your breath for however long you need to feel more centered and present. Release your day and get ready to connect. Take stock of how you're feeling emotionally and how you're feeling physically. Take note of it. That way you know what's already going on with you, and it's easier to recognize something new that isn't yours when connecting to your animal.

✦ Bring your awareness to your heart, and imagine a light emanating from your heart, connecting to your animal's heart. Take a moment to tell your animal how much you love them, and let them know that you'd love to have a conversation if they're open to it. You can invite them to share whatever is most important for them to share with you. If you're not getting much, you can also dive into your questions for them and be open to any responses you get.

✦ For a delayed conversation, you would follow the same steps as above, but instead of listening for responses in the moment, communicate the questions you have for the animal, and let them know you'd love for them to send you their responses in the next day or two. If you're doing this delayed method, it's best to keep your questions shorter, and ask only one or two questions per session, so you don't overwhelm the animal or yourself. For the rest of the day, make sure to be aware of anything that pops up out of the blue in response to your questions.

It is helpful to first take stock of your own emotions and your own physical body before you communicate with your animal companion. That makes you aware of what is already going on within yourself, so you aren't stuck wondering if what's coming through from your animal is actually something that you were already feeling personally. Was that pain in my elbow already there before I sat down to communicate or is it my cat's elbow pain that I am feeling? If you take stock of your own emotions and physical state first before you communicate with them, you can put your own issues to the side. If those same things come up in the session once you start communicating with them, and you haven't just let your mind wander, then it's likely your animal shares those same issues or wants to talk about those things.

In my experience, it's not uncommon that an animal and their human are dealing with similar issues. I've seen multiple times an animal diagnosed with a health problem that their human is dealing with. Some might wonder if our animals absorb our energy and therefore end up with our problems. I don't think that's the case. I think we just tend to be drawn subconsciously to others with similar problems or tendencies as us, including animal companions.

CHAPTER 2

Other Methods and Tips

I f you want to get a conversation going with another human, they will likely be a lot more willing and open to talking to you if you approach them warmly and with interest. The same goes for animals. We have to consider our own energy when we approach an animal for a conversation. If we come to the conversation feeling down and low and burdened in our own mind with all our own day-to-day problems, it's probably going to be a bit of a turnoff for an animal to communicate with us. If we come to them with an upbeat energy, with love and enthusiasm about our conversation, the animal is more likely to respond in kind.

There's a term you may have heard before that is somewhat common in modern spiritual circles: "raising your vibration." It's often used broadly to mean different things, but I believe there are two ways of understanding the term in our context: The first is that raising your vibration means working through your "issues" in the long term (for example, your grudges, your low self-esteem, any unreleased anger, etc.) to clear your energy field in a general sense. This often helps our readings because it makes us a clearer translator for an animal, and a clear energy field makes it easier to connect. This is, of course, a long journey that can take years and years—it isn't a simple process to work through a lot of the things that may be the source of a lowered vibration. I also don't think it's fully possible to work through *all* our "stuff." I think there will always be issues that we're dealing with personally, and we're all just human, after all, even if you do this work full time. Just because we do spiritually related work, that does not mean that we don't have flaws or personal challenges. But I do think it's helpful to make sure we're also developing ourselves personally alongside our animal communication abilities, since that can really help the work.

The second way of thinking about "raising your vibration" in our context is that it's about getting into a positive, upbeat, happy, "high-vibrational" energy before doing a reading, in the short term, to help you connect more effectively. An animal is much more likely to want to talk to me if I approach them with a loving, upbeat energy, or at the very least a neutral energy. It's also important to remember that because the information from the animal is filtered through the animal communicator, if I am in a bad mood or feeling negative that day, that is going to color the information coming through from the animal. That means I might naturally interpret the information coming through in a negative way, or miss some of the more positive aspects coming through. Additionally, if I go into the session feeling sorry for the animal and feeling sad about what they've been through, I can't be a clear channel for what they wish to communicate, because I've already made judgments and formulated thoughts about their experience that might not be true. Not only that, but it is easy to lose my focus if I get swept up in sadness. So a neutral or elevated mood helps me stay balanced and focused during the session as well.

You can be in a receptive, open state of awareness while at the same time being in a positive high-energy state—what we might call a "high-vibing" state. Earlier we talked about how, when doing animal communication, typically we're in a hypersensitive state, while at the same time trying to quiet the logical thinking brain. You can think of raising your vibration before a reading as "lifting your spirits" into that high-vibe, hypersensitive state. You can do this before a reading by, for example, dancing around, listening to uplifting music, or going for a walk in nature. If you're open to connecting to spirit guides, you can ask your guides to help you raise your vibration before you do a reading, too.

How to Approach a Reading

Here is my usual process: I like to make sure that I am in a state of upbeat, bright-eyed, bushy-tailed energy, and that I feel very curious about the animal I am about to connect to, and also open to hearing what's true for them. I make sure to set aside any preconceived ideas I have about the animal, and try to go into the session with as clear a slate as possible. Meditating before the session is helpful for letting go of my day-to-day issues and worries and helps me get centered, so I usually commit to a short meditation beforehand. If I have time after that, I try to put on some lively music to dance around to before the start of my session. That helps me get into a fun, excited, positive energy for my connection.

Two More Tools

There are a couple more tools you can use in a conversation, which can help deepen your connection and bring through more information from an animal. The first is more focused on personality and behaviors: During the reading, you can visualize yourself in the same room (or field) as the animal. Imagine yourself physically interacting with them. Notice: Do they come straight up to you? Maybe they're very sociable. Do they want to snuggle? Do they plop down and show their belly? Maybe belly rubs are their favorite thing. Do they swat you, do they show any fierceness? Do they act aggressively toward you? Do they shy away from you?

Just to be clear, the things they do when interacting with you like this through the visualization are not usually meant literally. Meaning, if you visualize yourself in a field with a horse, and they kick in your direction in the visualization, it does not mean that they want to attack you specifically, nor does it mean that they don't want to talk to you. It's just their way of showing you that they are generally aggressive toward humans, or just that they are the type to kick at others. Or they might show you how they typically like to interact with their human (and so you are the stand-in for their human in the example they show you). There have also been many times when I'm mid-conversation with an animal, connecting to them from across a distance from my home, and they will want to share with me what they're doing right then in that moment, or the thing that they are about to do. I might suddenly see them walking up the stairs, in my mind's eye. Or they might show me how itchy they are in their body during our session and want their human to scratch them immediately.

Extra information gleaned through the visualization can offer insights into the other topics they want to talk about, such as any behavioral issues they've been having. Let's say in this visualization exercise they show you very dominant behaviors and body language, and then later on in the reading they talk about how they're having some issues with other animals in the home. The fact that they already showed you they have a strong need to be dominant can help inform you about the root issues between them and the other animals.

The other wonderful thing about this method is that it also can be a great way to get a conversation going. After having connected heart to heart and having introduced yourself to the animal, if you then start visualizing yourself in the same space as them, information can start to flow from them much more easily. Our own brain is great at getting in the way of a conversation, especially if we're the ones trying to jump-start it. Using this visualization technique as a starting point can help conversation flow more easily.

The other technique for gleaning more information is called "merging bubbles." This is a method that is great for bringing through more information, especially related to how an animal is feeling in their body, and what it's like to be them. You get to experience them and their energy as if you were them. For this method, after you've already started communicating with the animal, you ask them if you can share energy with them so you can experience what it's like to be them. Then visualize yourself surrounded in a bubble of light, as well as the animal in their own separate bubble of light. Then, imagine those two bubbles merging into one. You can ask the animal if they can share their sight so that you can see through their eyes. Please note that you are not actually merging into one being. You're not possessing their body, and they're not possessing yours. This technique is more like an overlapping and sharing of energy. You are temporarily sharing the same energetic space, to briefly experience more of their perspective.

Don't overthink this exercise too much. Just focus on what you're experiencing in the moment, and analyze it later. It's also okay if you can't visualize the bubbles clearly. Know that the energy follows your intentions.

Exercise: Interacting in the Same Space and Merging Bubbles

Take a few deep breaths, feel yourself centered and grounded, and now bring your awareness to the center of your chest, to your heart center, feeling that light there big and bright. And now expand that light at the center of your chest, either through visualizing it emanating outward, or just setting the intention and knowing that the energy will follow. Visualize or feel that light from your heart expanding outward to connect to the animal's heart center, and, as you do so, send the animal lots and lots of love. Mentally introduce yourself to them, and ask if they'd be willing to help you develop your animal communication skills to be of better service to animals everywhere. Now I want you to mentally ask the animal to tell you about himself or herself. Notice anything and everything, no matter how it comes through to you, whether through images in your mind, sounds in your mind, or feelings in your body.

Ask the animal to give you a sense of what their personality is like. Try visualizing yourself in the room with them, or in a field together, and notice how they interact with you.

Now ask the animal if you can merge energy with them, so you can experience what it's like to be them. Visualize yourself surrounded in a bubble of light. Visualize them surrounded in their own bubble of light. And then visualize those bubbles merging or overlapping. As you merge energy with them, notice what it looks like to see out of their eyes. What things do you see? Are there any predominant colors in the room around them? Really feel what their/your body feels like. Do you notice any pain or tension anywhere in their body? It might come through feeling as if it were your own pain or tension. Notice any sounds around them. What other things can they tell you about themselves, such as their age, or things that they love, or things they hate? You might continue to experience communication through them, or it might begin to come through as separate impressions as it did when you first connected, such as thoughts, images, words, or feelings. Anything else the animal wants to show you about themselves, let them share that now.

When you're done, thank the animal for sharing with you and helping you. Visualize your bubbles separating again, and the light between your hearts dissolving.

Group Call

When I first started exploring animal communication, I joined a practice circle with others who also wanted to hone their animal communication skills. We exchanged photos of each others' animals online, so we could practice with them. I gave the rest of the group a photo of my cat Humphrey to connect to, and went off to meditate a bit while I waited for everyone's responses. They were going to connect to Humphrey, see what he wanted to talk about, and bring through some information about him to verify their connection with him. As I sat on my bed meditating, my other cat Gilly came into the room and jumped up onto the bed. She stared straight at me and in my head I heard a loud and clear "I just talked to some people!" as if Gilly were very proud of herself. My initial reaction was to shake it off and assume it was just my brain making things up. I knew Humphrey was the one who was supposed to be talking to the practice group, and his photo was the only one I had sent them. When I went to check everyone's responses to their connection with Humphrey, I could see, clear as day from the evidence, that, sure enough, they had all actually connected with Gilly instead, even if they only had Humphrey's photo and they had all intended to talk with him.

This is what I lovingly like to refer to as an animal hijacking a conversation. Or, rather, that animal communication really functions more like a group call in its essence. The heart-to-heart visualization I shared with you in the first part of this book is really helpful to set the intention of who we want to connect to, and it's a good way of establishing that connection. However, it is not quite as simple as calling from one cell phone to another cell phone. It's more like calling from one cell phone to someone's home phone so that everyone else who lives in that home can choose to pick up the receiver or listen in. If one of the people at home wants to join in and talk over the others, they certainly can. That means that other animals who live in the same home, connected to the same humans, might want to talk. This also includes animals that have passed on. One way I like to see it is as a web of energy connecting the client with all their animal companions, living and passed, and I am connecting to the animals through that web of energy.

Now it's normal to wonder if random animals walking by on the street can jump in on the conversation, too. Most likely they won't, because they're not part of that web of energy. But if the neighbor's dog is a good friend of the person you're doing a reading for, then certainly they are connected to that person's web of energy in some way, so that dog might want to jump in if they notice that there's a "phone line" open to communicate with one of their favorite people.

So if it is like a group call and a free-for-all in the home, how do you work with that so that it's not just chaos? Sometimes you might intend to connect to one animal, and another animal in the home responds. Sometimes you're mid-conversation with one animal, and another animal interrupts and wants to share their opinion on the matter, or they just want to talk about themselves. In general, I find it best to allow the animals to express themselves in whichever order they want. If I start trying to control the situation too much, I'll start getting in my own way and constricting the connection. Animals are going to do what animals are going to do. Your best bet is to go with the flow.

If you find that you're connecting to a different animal than you intended to, that's okay. There might be a good reason that particular animal wants to talk to you first. It might be because of their personality. Maybe they're more outgoing, more talkative, more dominant, or they like to be the center of attention. It might be because they are part of the issues going on in the home. Or maybe the animal you intended to talk to isn't as good a communicator as the one who interrupted, so you'll have a different animal speaking for them. And maybe they just have important things they want to express. I would allow the animal talking to me to get everything they want to express off their chest, before I then move on to the one I intended to connect to.

With multiple animals in the home, it is especially important to make sure you're bringing through verifiable evidence, so you know who is connecting when. Some animals insist on talking over each other, which makes it trickier for us to keep them straight. Usually, if you are mid-conversation with one animal, and all of a sudden you feel as if there's a different pace or rhythm to the information coming through, or if the information all of a sudden feels a little random or out of the blue, those are good signs that a different animal has jumped in. You can, of course, ask them all to please talk only one at a time, and let them know that everyone can get a chance to talk. They might listen, but the emphasis is on *might*. Asking nicely helps, but ultimately the group is going to do what they think is best, and we are simply their translators.

I often enjoy having multiple animals come through in my sessions, as it makes it more interesting for me. I also like knowing that out of a group of animals, there's bound to be at least one excellent communicator in there, and that's always a wonderful help. If I am having a hard time communicating with one animal in the home, I might ask one of the other animals to help out.

How to Navigate When a Different Animal Than Expected is Coming Through

✦ Try to not fight it or control it. That usually won't work.

✦ Try to get clarity—ask for more info from whoever is connecting, so you and their human know who is talking.

✦ What is this animal's message—what do they need to express?

✦ After bringing through that animal's message, move on to the one you intended to connect to.

If you want to do this work professionally and have a hard time keeping groups of animals straight, you could try the following tip. At the beginning of the reading, try connecting to each animal briefly, to get a sense of everyone's individual personalities and energy. Then mentally place them around yourself in space. For example, in a home with three animals you could place the first animal mentally to your left, the second in front of you, and the third to your right. This makes it easier to tell who is connecting when, throughout the reading. I call this "juggling animals." Let's say I am doing a reading for a client who has three cats. I will start off my connection opening up to all three of them, introducing myself and inviting them into the conversation, asking if they can all briefly introduce themselves to me so I know who is who. I might all of a sudden get a sense of anxiety and obsessive self-grooming. I will then check with the human that this makes sense in relation to the orange tabby, and I mentally place the orange tabby to my left side. I continue and ask one of the other cats to share some identifying info about themselves, and I might get a sense of one who is constantly asking for food, and meows incessantly while everyone is sleeping. I then check in with the human if this makes sense about the black cat, and mentally place that cat in front of me. I continue and ask the last cat to share with me who they are. I might suddenly get an image of a cat lying right on top of their human's chest, and a sense of this being their spot. After checking with the human that this makes sense about the last cat, I then mentally would place this cat to my right. Then throughout the reading, I take note of which direction around me I feel like the information is coming from, or in which direction I am feeling drawn.

If you use that technique, then you might find yourself going a little bit back and forth between the animals. You might feel drawn to the first animal for a few minutes, before one of the others catches your attention, before the first one wants to comment again. To me it can often feel like I am juggling animals, but as you get to know each animal in the session, it gets easier to tell who is talking when.

You might be surprised by which souls show up when you sit down to communicate. Sometimes an animal that passed decades ago wants to talk the most in a session, even if you were only intending on connecting to some living animals. Just this past year I had a session with a client who wanted to connect to her living cat and some human loved ones that had passed away. Very unexpectedly, a couple of cats she had way back in the 1970s showed up to the session too. Animal communication can be a great opportunity for some unexpected reunions. An animal that has been watching over you from the spirit world for a while might feel relieved and excited to finally have a chance to say hello to you again.

How to Navigate Several Animals Wanting to Come through at the Same Time

✦ Again, try to not fight or control it.

✦ Ask everyone to please only talk one at a time, and let them know that you will try to get to everyone.

✦ Try to familiarize yourself with who is who in the beginning. Get an overview at the very beginning of the reading of who you feel coming through initially (two or three things about each animal, enough to briefly identify who they are), and then mentally place them in space around you. That can help keep clear up who is where and what is coming from whom. Then see who wants to take the lead, and go with the flow of it.

If you are communicating with your own animals, and you want to be sure of who you're connecting to, ask them to share something about themselves to help identify who they are. Since you already know them, it's easy for you to verify who is connecting when.

Ethics

If we want to do animal communication for other people's animals, it's important to have our ethics in order, so that we don't do harm. Earlier in the book, we talked about letting the animal lead the conversation and also about bringing through verifiable evidence, especially when it comes to connecting to other people's animal companions. This is an ethical consideration, to make sure we are truly connecting to an animal, and to make sure we respect the animal as an equal participant in the conversation. So, for example, we might start off the session by asking the animal what they wish to talk about, letting them talk about whatever is most important to them, which also gives us the opportunity to bring through evidence of our connection, but it also respects the animal and gives them a chance to fully express themselves.

The other half of the session you might let the animal's human companion ask whatever questions they have for the animal. The great thing is that, usually in the first part of the session, the animal will have most likely already answered several of the questions, without the owner even needing to ask them, because the animal usually knows quite well what their human is wondering about. (Then again, sometimes animals will tiptoe around the issue and might not want to bring it up themselves. It very much depends on the animal and the situation.) The other great thing about the part of the session where the animal is leading the conversation is that it allows the animal to explain things from their point of view. If we go into a session already knowing what kind of issues the animal is dealing with, and also what the human thinks is the reason for it, it would be much harder for us not to bring those projections into the session. It would taint our perception of what's going on for the animal. Sometimes an animal will see things very differently from their human, and if they can present things as purely as possible from their own point of view, that is ideal.

Another factor that I have mentioned briefly is the issue of consent from the animal to communicate. Animal communication is a partnership between the communicator, the animal, and the animal's human. There is no conversation if one of the partners does not want to communicate. It is showing basic respect for the animal to ask them for permission to communicate. However, it's also important to seek permission or consent from the animal's human, if this animal isn't your own companion. In my experience, most animal communication with domesticated animals is more successful when everyone participates and consents. An animal that isn't our own companion will likely worry about talking with us if they know their human doesn't know about the communication.

Additionally, to make sure we are approaching animal communication as ethically as possible, it's important to be honest and open with people about the fact that animal communication is an art, not a science. It's especially important to note this for people who have no experience with animal communication. There's an odd idea floating around in the ether of society about anything that goes under the heading of psychic or intuitive abilities: that when we are connecting, we are as a default always right about everything. Unfortunately, the fact is that there's a lot of room for misinterpretation in a reading, and we as animal communicators are fallible. Therefore, animal communication can never be a substitute for veterinary care, or proper training, or the right diet. We can never diagnose, nor can we prescribe.

When it comes to health, animal communication can help describe symptoms, and identify how the animal is feeling in their body. It can also be helpful in seeing what treatments the animal feels have been beneficial so far. It can offer insight into what kind of treatments the animal is open to and willing to move forward with. You might even see if you can get a clear sense of what's going on for them health-wise. However, you also have to be clear with the humans that you could be misinterpreting, and encourage them to go see a veterinarian regardless of what comes up in a reading.

Animal Wisdom

Animals come into our lives not only to share friendship and life experiences, but also to teach us things, and to help us through challenging times as we help them through the same. In my own experience, most animal companions carry a wealth of deep wisdom and accurate insights into us and into life in general. Don't forget: Your animals are often picking up on your thoughts, and are privy to the bigger things going on in our life that you may be struggling with. I often find that our animal companions love to share their insights, encouragement, and guidance, if they are given a chance.

What kinds of guidance would an animal share with their human? It could truly be about anything. It could be from the wisdom that they've accumulated on their own throughout their life. It could be wisdom and guidance about topics they've noticed their humans struggling with. Perhaps your animal would encourage you to connect with your inner child. They might push you to follow your passion, if you have been putting it off. Guidance on low self-esteem and body image is another topic that might come up. Healthy boundaries. Reminders to take care of yourself rather than only taking care of others. Self-love. Compassion. The necessity of slowing down. The benefits of playing more. Animals are surprisingly perceptive and tuned in to our inner worlds, and it might be worth taking the time to see what thoughts they might have on your life or situation.

A little while ago I connected to a client's three cats, all of whom were having some trouble adjusting to their new living arrangements. They had recently gone from being a two-cat household to a three-cat household, and the transition was a source of stress for them all. I connected to each one to see how they each saw the situation, and what things they felt could help improve it. After we worked through the situation with the first two cats, I connected with the smallest cat, who hadn't really shared much about herself yet. Once she decided to open up, she shared with me that she was a bit on the quieter side, and just along for the ride most of the time, taking the older cat's lead. She told me about some of her loves (food) and also that she was aware of how this impacted the dynamic among all the cats negatively, as she kept stealing the other cats' food. In terms of her personality, she was silly, quirky, and also a bit scatterbrained. But she wanted to make a point that she had a lot of wisdom within her as well. She proceeded to share that her human had recently been having a hard time just relaxing. That her human is so used to being super-productive all the time, that it was hard for her to just fully relax and be present. She offered to help her human with this, and her human acknowledged that that was something she was had recently been struggling a lot with. She was taking a break from work and had been fighting the constant urge to make her time off more productive, instead of just resting.

This is just one example of many things your animal companions can pick up on from your energy field and thoughts. You don't even have to tell them these things out loud. Even the animals you don't expect to be quite so perceptive may be more clued in to your life than you realize. If you take a moment to listen to them, you might gain some important insights and guidance.

Exercise: Ferreting Out Animal Wisdom

You can do this exercise with your own animal companions, or even try it with wildlife in the neighborhood if you're feeling adventurous. This is a good exercise for releasing any worries about being correct, as there's less pressure about what might come through. Try to see this as an exercise in allowing yourself to open up to the guidance from the animal, and expressing gratitude for it. They might share something about an issue you're already working on, or they might give you unexpected wisdom about something else that they personally have a lot of insight on.

Breathe, expand your energy, connect heart to heart with the animal, and send them lots of love, asking if you can connect with them to communicate. If you are connecting to an animal who isn't your own companion, tell them that you are an animal communicator looking to improve your abilities, and would they be so kind as to help you by communicating with you. Showing humility really helps. Then you might ask them to please share what wisdom or guidance they have for you individually. Acknowledge whatever comes through your psychic senses. When you're done, remember to thank them for their wisdom, and see the connection dissolving.

Animal Spirit Guides

Not only are we surrounded by living animals, but we are also surrounded by animals in spirit form—some who take on the role of spirit guides. *Spirit guides* is a term I use loosely to mean a category of spiritual, non-physical beings who take an interest in our well-being, and who wish to help us reach our full potential. Animal spirit guides fall under that same category. Some are present throughout our entire life, or at least for very long periods of time, while others appear for just a brief period to help us through particular phases or challenges.

Animal spirit guides typically help us to develop certain qualities that might be useful for us, that we might need for an upcoming situation in our life. For example, we might see that someone has a squirrel as an animal spirit guide for the moment, because maybe that person needs to work on gathering their resources, maybe saving money, and preparing for a metaphorical "winter." This kind of message is directly linked to what we know about squirrels: that they literally gather and hoard food to save for when resources are scarce in the winter. But the guidance an animal spirit has for a person doesn't always have to do with the general characteristics of that animal. It could be that we see a squirrel for someone, but that squirrel is helping them with something completely different, like self-esteem. That animal spirit guide will try to communicate that to us if we're doing an animal spirit guide reading, to clarify exactly what the guidance is for that person. So its presence might be directly linked to the general characteristics of the animal, or it might be something seemingly unrelated.

Can animals who have passed become our animal spirit guides? Yes, some do start to step into that role of helping their humans out from the spirit world, while some are busy with other things. We'll talk more about this later in the book.

Exercise: Reaching Out to Your Animal Spirit Guide

If you are still not sure about this concept of spirit guides and animal spirit guides, suspend your disbelief temporarily and just try it out. You can choose to see this as more practice with your psychic senses if you'd like.

Close your eyes, take a few deep breaths, and relax into the surface beneath you. I want you to see yourself standing in a waterfall of divine light. See or feel that waterfall of light washing over your body. See it washing away any negative energy, any tension or stress from the day, any fears or doubts about your abilities . . . see it all wash away . . .

Now I want you to see or feel yourself walking along a pathway through the forest. Notice how the ground feels beneath your feet. Notice the sound of the breeze blowing through the trees. Notice how the sun warms your skin . . .

Up ahead on the path, there is a door. Behind this doorway is a unique landscape where one of your animal spirit guides is waiting for you. I want you to walk up to this door, open it, and step inside, into this new landscape. What do you notice there? What animal is waiting for you there? Maybe you see more than one. It's okay if you can't seem to settle on one—that just means there are several there. Which is the most prominent? Connect with that one. What meaning does the animal hold? You may ask the animal to show you what guidance it has for you. If it isn't immediately clear, ask the animal to clarify, to show you what the meaning is. They might act it out for you, or just give you one key word, or they might give you an emotion. Be open to it all.

When you're ready, thank your animal spirit guide for helping guide you on your path. And when you're ready, you can bring your awareness back to your body, back to the room, and open your eyes. Write down your experience, even if it doesn't make sense right now. Include as many details as you can remember. You can come back to it at a later time and see if the guidance makes sense in hindsight.

Additional Tips

Here are some frequently asked questions from aspiring animal communicators:

Q: *When doing readings for others, should I connect to the animal first, write out what comes through from the animal, send that to the animal's human, and get feedback afterward? Or is it better if I connect to the animal live, with the human there giving me feedback in the moment?*

A: This is always up to the individual animal communicator, what they feel the most comfortable with. There are pros and cons to each method. When connecting live, with the human giving feedback in the moment, there's more of a chance of getting distracted. Many also feel extra pressure to perform in the moment. However, you also get feedback on the spot, which can boost your confidence, and you can course-correct and work through any misinterpretation you might have made at that moment. It also gives you the chance to troubleshoot with the animal's human and discuss any behavioral challenges the animal has. The animal's human also gets a chance to ask clarifying questions while you are connecting, which helps you make sure that everyone is on the same page.

When connecting to the animal on your own—writing the information down and sending it to their human, and then getting feedback later—there's less pressure to perform on the spot, and there are generally fewer distractions. However, it can be tough not to have immediate feedback that lets you know if you are connecting to the right animal, or if you're interpreting the communication correctly. It's much easier to doubt yourself and your connection when it's just you there, which will affect your ability to focus and communicate.

In general, I recommend that people try it out both ways. If you've done it only one way in the past, you will naturally feel that the other way is uncomfortable, but often it's just about what we're used to doing. We might feel that it's scary either way.

I personally favor the method of connecting live in the moment to the animal, and checking in with the human throughout the session to make sure that I am connecting correctly (through the evidence that comes through), that what I am saying makes sense, and that we're all on the same page. For me, it's the most practical way of doing a session for a client.

Q: *Doing sessions from a distance (over the phone or on a video call with the human) seems easier than in-person sessions—there's less temptation to be "distracted" by the physical presence of the animal. What can you suggest to help me be more centered and present during in-person sessions, and less distracted?*

A: Getting distracted by an animal's presence is definitely a big part of doing in-person sessions. I can't count the number of times I've had to connect through barking, excited invitations to play, puppies chewing on my hands, or a dog doing some spontaneous squirrel chasing. A dog even peed on my sweater once, mid-session, to mark my stuff as his territory. On the flip side, I can't count the number of times I've gotten to communicate while petting the client's animal companions, having them voluntarily sit in my lap and snuggle, or have them stare into my eyes for the session. My favorite part of doing readings in person with animals is the potential snuggles that I get to have with them. If you love animals, I would definitely say the snuggles are a major job perk.

If you tend to get easily distracted when trying to connect, I would recommend that you practice doing readings at a distance from your own home, with your eyes open first. This will help you get used to dealing with visual distractions alone while connecting. What I usually recommend to start is a session where you keep your eyes open, but look at a blank wall while connecting. Then, you should move on to looking out the window while you are communicating with the animal. If you are in person, you might try not looking at the animal directly. If a lot is going on around me in a session, I might go back and forth between keeping my eyes open and closing them if I need to focus more. Often, I am staring off into space or looking in the opposite direction of the animal when I do a reading.

You can also ask the client for their help in creating an environment with minimal distractions. But, when working with animals, you should always expect some kind of distraction. Ironically, over the years I feel that I have become more and more easily distracted. I try to give my clients a little heads-up about that when they schedule with me, that I prefer if they can try to make sure we're connecting at a quieter time of day in the home, or if they can limit the amount of activity in the home as much as possible. I encourage them to make sure the animal has just eaten, if possible, and ideally had some exercise already if they tend to be very excitable.

Doing sessions in person does give us a bit more information to start with, which could actually be an impediment. We as animal communicators have to work extra hard to ensure we're not making assumptions based on what we see with our own physical eyes in the session. The behavior we witness in the animal when we meet them could be a true behavior for them, or it could be something they never do, and therefore it may be misleading. If you do sessions in person with another human's animal companion, you have to be aware that an animal's behavior while you're there might be exactly what they always do, or it might be highly uncharacteristic for them. For example, they might be so nervous about the session (maybe feeling their human's anxiety about it, too), that they start behaving erratically. I have also heard clients exclaim how unusually calm or friendly their animal is when I come to our session. It's easy for our brain to assume that their behavior is their normal mode of operating, when maybe it's not. Make sure you don't make assumptions before you sit down to connect and communicate with them.

Q: *I feel like my brain likes to add in extra details that aren't from the animal's communication. How do I better handle that or how do I keep that from happening?*

A: I think it helps to know that it's normal for our brain to want to jump in and add useless stuff in a reading. It's normal for the brain to fill in some details that aren't from the animal, because it likes to get a complete overview when analyzing something. For example, very often in beginners I see that if the animal wants to talk about a favorite couch they love to lie on, the beginner's brain will add a color to the couch, but the color is wrong because it wasn't something the animal shared. The animal just wanted to talk about the couch, but wasn't focusing on the color (never mind that many animals see color differently from us). It's okay that the brain automatically adds in details—as long as we are aware of that habit and can learn to navigate it.

In a situation like the one above, with an animal wanting to talk about their favorite spot, I might tell the client, "The dog is showing me their absolute favorite spot is the couch. Does that make sense to you?" Then, if I am not sure about the details, I might say, "For some reason it's coming through to me as a bright red couch. I'm not sure if that's significant or not, or if she just wants to talk about a couch in general." So here I am pacing myself by first focusing on the most important part of what the animal shared with me (loving to lie on the couch), and I check with the human about it, and then I continue and acknowledge how it came through to me and add in the detail if I am not sure whether it's significant or not.

When you get a lot of information from an animal about something all at once, you can take a moment to lean in to which aspect it feels that the animal wants to emphasize. Then you go from there to see if the added details make sense or not. If not, then those were likely added by your own brain. That's okay. With practice it gets easier to tell which things the animal is emphasizing, and which things are just added noise from your brain, trying to fill in the picture. In a similar vein, we can often misinterpret or jump to conclusions based on the information coming through. That doesn't mean you're not connecting. You may have just misinterpreted. For example, when an animal shows me they have very youthful energy, I could jump to the conclusion that that means they are very young, or it could just mean they have youthful energy but are actually quite old. If you find that your readings tend to be a little bit hit-or-miss, with half the information making sense to the human and half of it not making sense at all, make sure you pace yourself, make sure you're not rushing to conclusions, and make sure you take time to intuitively investigate what the animal seems to be emphasizing.

✦

PART TWO

Animal Beings

CHAPTER 3

Animal Behavioral Challenges and Health Challenges

Behavioral Challenges

What is a behavioral challenge? In human-animal companionships, the reality is that the animal has to do a lot of adjusting to their human's lifestyle, and the human has to adjust to the animal's needs. Sometimes the two clash and the animal's needs aren't being met or there is some miscommunication going on, and that then leads to behavioral issues. A behavioral challenge is essentially a behavior that an animal does that either causes harm to themselves or others, a destructive habit causing harm to their environment, or a behavior that is deeply annoying to those around them, making it hard to live with them or take care of them. It could be as serious as showing aggression to other animals or humans, or as destructive as peeing inside the house, or as annoying as jumping on people to greet them. It might be that the animal is really vocal, putting everyone around them on edge. It could be a horse that kicks in the direction of their people so no one is able to groom them and take care of their health. Generally, you could say that a behavioral challenge is any kind of unwanted behavior.

The biggest mistake I see people make is that they take their animal's challenging behaviors personally. It's really tempting to assume that the animal does an annoying behavior to spite us, when actually, in most cases, animals just have a need that they are trying to meet and they don't know any other way to get that need met. Sometimes animals even think they're being helpful by doing the behavior.

When you take a behavior personally, you're letting your emotions muddle your connection and your communication with your animal. It can also start to erode your relationship. That then might lead to a vicious cycle where your emotions about the behavior cause your animal companion to become extra anxious, leading to more of the unwanted behavior, or introducing a new unwanted behavior, due to the increased anxiety.

It's helpful to remember that there are many possible reasons an animal performs a behavior. First of all, it might be because the animal has a specific need or desire that they're trying to meet, including an instinctual need. All animals have various needs, depending on the type of animal they are, as well as their own individual personality and life needs. A cat who likes to be close to their human might want to sit on the kitchen counter to get higher up and meet that need. Or a cat who is territorial might like to scratch the furniture to meet their need to mark the space as theirs.

Secondly, an animal might have been trained to do the behavior. Unfortunately, we humans tend to train our animals to do an unwanted behavior without realizing it. You might see this in the case of a very vocal, demanding cat that meows for their dinner, and then we feed them their food mid-meow, and then the cat starts to link those two together: They meow, and we give them food. Then any time of day that they feel hungry for a snack, they will use incessant meowing to try to communicate that, because it has worked in the past. Or let's say a dog starts to bark at other dogs on walks as a way to express their excitement. We might start to hold the leash tighter and tense up every time we see another dog. Our dog feels that, and then that encourages them to worry about other dogs and become more reactive toward them. Animals who have been encouraged (even if we didn't mean to encourage them) to perform an annoying behavior might be confused and even think they're doing a great job by doing the behavior.

Thirdly, the animal might be reacting to something that is triggering a deeper fear or anxiety in them, and then the behavior is the only way they know how to express or handle that fear or anxiety. This might underlie the actions of a dog who chews on the furniture when left home alone, because they are anxious without their humans there. The dog might not know any other way of handling their anxiety. A behavior is never done out of spite and it's never personal. Even in the case of a cat who poops on your clothes when you come home from a long trip away. That's the only way they know how to express their displeasure with you being gone. It's not that they want to be a pain in the neck, nor is it about revenge for them.

Finally, it's hugely important to remember that behavioral issues are sometimes actually related to health issues, so it's always helpful to make sure your animal companion has been to the vet, if they start to exhibit odd or worrying behaviors.

When people take the first steps toward bringing an animal into their family, they often have an idealized vision of what having an animal companion will look like in their head. I totally get that it may be frustrating when that vision doesn't materialize. Or maybe the person has spent a lot of money and time to try to change the behavior, but it hasn't worked. It can be heartbreaking, especially when it's a behavior that causes harm to the animal themselves or others. Our personal feelings about the situation can often get in the way of us being able to hear and understand the animal clearly, because our emotions drown out the subtle communication from the animal. If you have been struggling with behavioral challenges with your animal companions, make sure you're putting your own feelings to the side for now, in order to approach them and your communication on the best foot possible.

Also, most importantly, make sure you are nurturing your bond with them. Those animals who have a strong bond with you will feel more incentive to modify their behavior. An animal with a strong bond will be much more responsive to their human than an animal who does not have a strong bond with their human.

To summarize, when working with your own animals: Don't take it personally, put your feelings to the side to be as open as possible to what the animal needs, and make sure to nurture your bond with them. When working with other people's animals, encourage their humans to do the same.

Sometimes an animal will change a behavior after just having a conversation about it. However, most often the situation will require a mix of training, behavior modification, and changing the environment to set the animal up for success. This is why, even if animal communicators are not trainers or behaviorists, it's definitely helpful for us to read up on these topics, so that we have some tools or experts we can direct people to if we feel that these things might be helpful in that particular situation. You can even get a sense of whether a certain method of training might be helpful or not, for that particular situation and animal, using your intuitive abilities. You can run the suggestion by the animal and see if they'd be open to it.

How Do You Work with Behavioral Challenges in a Session?

When working through behavioral challenges, the first step is to get a sense of why the animal does the behavior. What needs are they trying to meet? What is this behavior linked to? Do they feel that their behavior is helpful? Do they do it just for fun or because it benefits them in some way? Are they confused about it? Is it a compulsive behavior for them? Is it rooted in anxiety or fear of something? Does it stem from a past trauma or event? Or is it more related to how they're doing health-wise? Do they have pain or is something else going on, causing them to behave this way?

Even just getting a sense of *why* an animal does a behavior can help us find ways to work with the animal to where the behavior benefits everyone. I had a client a while ago who hired me to talk to her rescued birds, and to work with one particular dove's behavioral challenges. In this case, the challenging behavior was a combination of the dove's personality and instinctual behavior creating an annoyance for his humans. The following is her experience, in her own words:

The first time you came to my house, you talked to a Eurasian collared dove named Handsome. He was driving me crazy by always trying to drive me to his nest. You told me he was very intelligent and that he felt as if he was helping us with this behavior. I asked if he wanted to be released. You told me that was scary for him. He wanted to transition to an aviary with other birds, but he needed help to do that. He also said he needed a job to do to keep him occupied and out of trouble, because of how smart he was. A little bit later I met a woman in the Seattle area who had some little diamond doves, a few pigeons, and was becoming interested in rehab. She fell in love with Handsome and I let her take him home. It was a relief for me and also very sad. He started doing all the things to her he did to me, such as bossing her around and getting into everything.

Handsome had a cage in the dove room. He was out most of the day and in the evening she would let the little doves out to fly around. One evening she went into the room to round them up and put them in their individual cages, but they were already in their cages ready for the cage door to be closed. She was amazed because usually it was quite an ordeal to get them back in their cages. The next night, the same thing happened. All the doves were in their cages.

One evening, she went to the dove room earlier than usual and watched as Handsome flew into each cage, vocalized, and the doves who lived in the cage got inside. He continued with each cage until each dove was inside. Handsome gave himself a job that used his strengths to be helpful! He eased up on his bossy behaviors with his humans after that.

The reasoning behind an animal's behavior can give us a sense of how to approach the situation. If the behavior is anxiety-based, then just telling the animal what we'd like them to do most likely is not going to be enough. We need to address the anxiety. If the animal is using the behavior to try to meet a need, then how can their human meet those needs for the animal in a way that works for everyone? The question about whether or not behavior is compulsive can be helpful to give you a sense of what might be needed to help shift the behavior. In my experience, it's a spectrum. Some animals might perform a behavior in a very compulsive way, to the point that they have no control over it and they need help from their human by removing all temptations that could lead to the behavior. Others might do a behavior, and it's just slightly compulsive, but they can rein it in with the right incentive. Some animals do a behavior because they thought they were supposed to, but there's no inkling of compulsion there, and explaining to them what you'd love for them to do instead might be enough for them to change.

After getting a sense of why the animal does a behavior, we can explain to them why that behavior is problematic from the human's perspective. We then can share what behavior we're actually hoping for, and why. You might ask them what they need in order to reach that goal. Do they need their humans to change their environment, to support them in changing their behavior? Do their humans need to change their own behaviors or habits to support them? Does the animal need incentives? Would training be something that could help encourage them to move in the right direction? If so, what kinds of training have they tried, what has been helpful, and what hasn't? You might suggest some types of training to the animal and see how open they are to trying that out.

Possible Reasons Behind an Animal's Behavioral Challenges

✦ Sometimes the animal thinks they're supposed to do the behavior, that it's helpful or wanted. Often their humans have unwittingly trained their animal to do the behavior, but it could be a random behavior they picked up as well.

✦ The behavior is instinctual (related to the type of animal they are, or sometimes their breed or personality).

✦ The animal does the behavior out of fear or anxiety. The behavior is the only way they know how to deal with their anxiety. The behavior could stem from a specific past trauma or event, or from a more general sense of anxiety. Some animals come into the world on high alert, whereas others are born more mellow.

✦ The behavior could be related to how the animal is feeling physically in their body (if they have pain somewhere, for example). You should always check in with the vet if your animal starts to exhibit any new concerning behavior.

✦ Sometimes there's no reason other than the fact that the animal derives some joy or benefit from doing the behavior, and they haven't been presented with the right incentives to stop.

A communication tool that I have found very helpful in my sessions is reframing. Honestly, it's often the key to many behavioral challenges, especially when the behavior is grounded in anxiety or fear, or if the animal just doesn't see any reason to do the preferred behavior. Reframing is essentially when you try to shift their perspective on the issue at hand, and help them see the new positive behavior as something they will benefit from in the long run. With anxiety-based behaviors, you are reframing the scary situations as something more benign and positive. For example, if the animal is scared of inanimate objects like trash cans or washing machines (you'd be surprised how many times I've encountered this), I would explain to the animal how benign those objects are, no matter how freaky they might have seemed in the past. I might explain to the animal how that object actually helps us and that their humans love having it around. I might show them that it's safe to relax around the object, and I might show them that the ultimate goal is for them to be able to spend time near that object while feeling completely safe and confident.

Even behaviors that are not rooted in fear or anxiety can benefit from reframing. Let's say a younger cat in the home has been trying to engage an older, grumpier cat in a playtime routine, but it's been too much for the older cat, so he's been striking out at the youngster. I would show the younger cat how giving the older cat more space will make him much more amenable to becoming friends over time. I might encourage the younger cat to find toys to play with, and that might be a better way of inviting the older one to play. I am reframing the new behavior I am hoping to encourage as something that will ultimately lead to better results for the youngster.

With reframing, it's also helpful to phrase the new behavior for the animal in a way that appeals to their personality or needs. If a dog loves to show off how amazing he is, and loves to be praised as the best dog in the world, then it might be a good idea to share with him how impressed his humans will be if he starts doing the new preferred behavior, and how it helps him be a good role model for others.

Reframing is also beneficial for the animal's human to consider and use for themselves. What often happens, especially with fear- or anxiety-based behaviors, is that the human will start to take on some of those fears or anxieties themselves. Let's take the case of a dog reacting aggressively to other dogs on walks. The human may not have started off as worried about other dogs, but once they've had several stressful encounters like this, they start to dread meeting other dogs on walks, because they know how their own dog will react. This is the type of thing that creates a vicious cycle, where their dog then picks up on their human's dread of other dogs, and becomes even more reactive. So not only is it important to reframe the situation for the animal, but also for the human. We need to go from thinking that every dog we meet is a potential trigger, to thinking that every dog we meet is a potential friend, so that our dog isn't picking up on any unnecessary anxiety from us. The human might have to actively demonstrate this belief to their dog by pointing out every dog they meet from far away and saying joyfully, "Look, there's another potential dog friend!" Will this cure the situation fully? Probably not, but it's an important step in shifting the animal's perspective on it.

I always make sure that I end a conversation on behaviors by sending the animal a clear picture of what the ideal situation is, clarifying what the goal is and what that actually looks like. That way I am not leaving them with any confusion on which direction we're hoping they'll go. I find it helpful for the animal's humans to make sure they're giving their animal reminders after the session, by stating the preferred behavior, by visualizing it, and by restating anything that we reframed in the session. If you are the animal's human, then even if you have already talked your animals through these issues once, it's still a good idea to give them reminders in the future.

It's important to remember that you're dealing with individuals—and that doesn't just refer to the animals, but also the humans. Animal communication isn't about forcing an animal to do anything. You are working *with* the animal to find a solution that works for everyone. You're not trying to "fix" the animal. It's about finding solutions together, it's about creating understanding between them and their human, and it's about creating harmony between the two. I often imagine that this work is very much like what I suspect being a marriage counselor is like. You need to have compassion and understanding for both sides, and hear both sides out, before you can find a solution that works for both of them.

Sometimes the session has been so therapeutic to the animal that they make remarkable efforts toward shifting their behavior, even before their human gets a chance to make any changes themselves. Just the fact that their human went through the effort of scheduling a session with an animal communicator, or their human took the time to sit down themselves to communicate, can mean so much to the animal. Just the opportunity to express themselves fully can be very therapeutic. It would not be surprising to me if you see small shifts in your relationship just from taking the time to listen to them.

Very rarely, an animal's behavioral challenge will not have a clear solution to it that can be met by their current humans. Sometimes that does mean that re-homing is the best solution for everyone. Let's take the example of a cat who was feral, who now lives indoors and poops everywhere. The cat might do this because she is so displeased with having to be inside all the time and wants the freedom to come and go as she pleases. The cat's humans might live in an apartment on the fifth floor and don't have any way of letting the cat go outside. There are, of course, things that could be done to see if the cat could be made content and happy inside, such as enriching the environment so much that she's never bored. However, if the humans have exhausted all tools and options with no improvement, it's possible that the best solution for everyone involved would be to find another loving home for the cat where she can have access to the outdoors.

Please note that re-homing is an absolute last-ditch solution, and not at all the first thing I jump to in a session. It is extremely difficult to re-home an animal, as there are already so many animals out there needing a home, and it's extremely stressful for an animal to move from home to home (not to mention, from family to family). Do we first try to see if there's a solution where everyone is happy first? Yes, no question. Typically I don't recommend re-homing at all. My job as the animal communicator is to acknowledge what the animal's needs and desires are, and from there I see how they and their humans can work together to meet those needs and desires. If some of the animal's needs are non-negotiable, and their humans can't meet those needs, then it may be a good idea to see if there is someone out there who can. I have talked to many animals who have finally come to the perfect-fit family, with people who were able to take care of their non-negotiable needs. Had they stayed in their previous homes, they would not have thrived as they do now. That said, in my work it's rare to come by completely non-negotiable needs that the animal's humans can't meet. Luckily, some creative problem solving is enough in most cases.

To sum up, the following are the possible reasons an animal does a certain behavior, and below that are the steps to talk an animal through their behavioral challenges.

How Animal Communication
Can Address Behavioral Challenges

Reason: Why does the animal do this, and what needs are they trying to meet? Explaining this to the human. Spectrum of compulsive versus not compulsive, instinctual versus not, to give you a sense of how responsive they might be to you just talking them through it, and to give you a sense of how much training might be helpful to prompt them to change their behavior.

Explaining: Explaining to the animal what we actually want and why.

Training: What extra tools and training might be helpful in reaching the ideal situation?

Compromising: What might the human have to do to help their animal through it?

Reframing: Shifting the animal's perspective on the trigger/ issue, phrasing it in a way that appeals to their personality/ needs. Showing them how it benefits them in the long run. Hugely beneficial for the animal's human to consider and use themselves, so as not to create a vicious cycle.

Ideal situation: Making clear what the goal is and what that actually looks like. Let them know it's a goal, and it's OK if we're not always perfect, as long as we're making efforts to reach our goal.

Here's an example from a client I had a couple of years ago. During his session with his three cats, we went into each cat's personality, as well as each cat's likes, dislikes, needs, and wants. Through this information, he got some pointers from each of them on how to make some small tweaks in order to increase everyone's happiness and the general harmony in the home.

> We have three cats—Ben, Lucy, and Gigi. They're all so different and have such unique personalities, and Thea offered us the opportunity to get into their heads to improve their lives, and ours. Ben is a nervous boy. He'd often run away from groups, and had trouble sitting still. During our session with Thea, she told us we need to verbally reiterate to Ben how brave he is. Now, every day (and it has been almost two years) we tell Ben, "You're so brave, Ben!" His demeanor has notably improved. He loves groups, he can snuggle with people he's just met, and he loves to be around people. He needed to know we acknowledged his growth, and I'm so glad Thea showed us that.

> Lucy is a constant crier. She loves to play in our yard (which she can't get out of) and particularly loves to spend time with the next door neighbor's cat. Problem is, she'll cry until she gets what she wants, like going outside. Thea showed us that if we acknowledge Lucy while she's quiet, she'll start to associate being quiet with getting what she wants. This small tweak has been a complete game changer for us.

Gigi, well that's my baby! It was interesting to hear that Gigi doesn't care that Ben and Lucy are around. We had Ben and Lucy for three years before getting Gigi, and immediately Gigi became the star child. (She's also the only one who doesn't constantly vomit, so that definitely makes it easier.) Being around her two dads is the true joy of her life, and Thea confirmed that with us. Gigi told us through Thea that being offered people food is the source of joy in her life that we need to constantly give. Any time we cook, we offer Gigi a small bite, even if she doesn't actually want it (which she usually doesn't, as she only likes cream-based foods). She just needs to know the people food is being offered to her. It's a way that helps her feel more human and closer to us. We now have a stroller for her and a travel backpack so we can take her on hikes.

I can't recommend animal communication enough! Our session with Thea was a birthday gift, and seriously impacts us to this day, two years later.

Discord in the Multi-Animal Home

If you've ever lived with more than one animal at the same time, you know it's not just their relationships with you that are important. Their relationships with each other can make or break the harmony in the home for everyone who lives there. I work a lot with groups of animals, and it can be tough when there are wildly different personalities that don't go well together, and different species of animals that have very different body languages and needs. In some homes, the discord between animals might be subtle, with animals expressing their discontent in a passive-aggressive way, such as destroying their environment as a way of marking their territory, or lying in the middle of a tight hallway, poised to lash out, so nobody feels safe walking by them. The signs may also be less than subtle, though, and include full-out fights between the animals who are not getting along.

Whenever we're talking about the dynamics between animals, it's helpful to talk about their views of the hierarchy within the home. It seems to me that most animals have a sense of hierarchy, of who is in charge of whom, who gets their opinions respected, and who gets first pick when it comes to coveted sleeping spots or toys. Some animals view themselves as on the same level—or above—their humans in the hierarchy. These are the animals who have the "I do what I want, thank you very much" type of mentality.

An animal viewing himself at the top of the hierarchy of the animals in the home is not necessarily a problem, and especially not if the other animals are happy to let that one take the lead. Some animals feel safe having a dominant leader around. Those kinds of animals thrive as a follower and would feel rudderless and anxious in a position of power. In general, animals have a tendency to figure out their hierarchy themselves and easily fall into a spot that feels natural for them. But it can be a problem if you have multiple dominant personalities in a household, or if the dominant animal takes everyone else's behavior as a personal challenge to their spot at the top. Additionally, things get easily shaken up in the hierarchy any time there's a big change in the family, whether it's an addition, a changing of homes, or when an animal passes away. Some who were lower down in the hierarchy might see a change in their environment as their chance to stage a coup d'état and take over as head of the animal family.

As always, we want to make sure we get a clear sense of how the animals feel about each other, and why they are behaving the way they are. Did something happen between the animals that caused a rift? Did they never really get a chance to bond? The animal that tends to start trouble might naturally have a very dominant personality, or there might be multiple animals who are naturally very dominant and want to be at the top of the hierarchy. It could just be a clashing of personalities. Some might feeler safer as the head, because of their past: Maybe they were picked on by others, so now they try to assert themselves aggressively in the hierarchy as a way to feel safe. Some animals might have such intense anxiety that they redirect that to the animals around them. Remember that health issues can always be at the root of behaviors like this, too, so it's important to make sure the animals get checked out by a vet if these kinds of struggles are happening.

Once we understand each animal's way of thinking, their reasoning and perspective on the situation, we can be much better informed about how to talk them through the situation. When we find what needs they are trying to fulfill with this behavior, we can see how those needs can be fulfilled in a different way. If they are asserting themselves aggressively because this is the only way they know how to feel in control and safe in the situation, then we want to work on their feelings of safety in the home in addition to seeing what changes we can make in their environment to foster that feeling of safety. We can also use this opportunity to talk them through their anxieties about control.

If the animal is very focused on wanting more space or if they've been very territorial, I might find different ways to make sure they at least feel that that they have more space. That might mean they get more time outdoors, or maybe there's a way to build more space vertically in the home, such as adding more cat trees for cats. If they're territorial, I would find ways to allow them to mark their space in an appropriate way, such as with scratching posts, or I might encourage them to rub against objects to mark their space.

As you continue to communicate with the animal, you'll move on to the explanation for why a different situation is needed. This is a good opportunity to reframe the new situation for the animal. I often choose to share a desire for every member of the family to feel safe and comfortable in the home, including them. I explain that that means the animals of the home, as well as the humans, will need to work together to create that harmony, which will mean being more generous and kind to one another. I might talk the animal through a more harmonious idea of the hierarchy in the home, perhaps introducing the concept of a horizontal hierarchy where everyone gets to feel confident and have their needs met. In this situation, everyone can feel safe and comfortable. More dominant animals can be on top of the hierarchy without constantly needing to assert themselves. In this case, it's possible for them to shift into calm confidence instead of anxious control.

If their lashing out comes from a place of wanting to control others, I might help the animal see how futile that effort is, how everyone and everything around them is likely going to change and shift throughout their lives, and how ultimately we can only control ourselves and work on going with the flow. I might investigate what could help them get to that point of going with the flow. Do they need more exercise and play? What things can their human do to help?

When reframing the situation for the animal, it's really helpful to encourage them to see the bigger benefit of having the other animal companions around. I emphasize that they are potential friends and allies, potential playmates or snuggle companions. I remind the animal that even if they're not interested in having friends right now, the other animals in their home can still offer great emotional support when the humans go out for the day or leave for a vacation. If the animal is still not able to get to the point of seeing the positive possibilities, that is totally fine. If that happens, I might encourage them to just ignore each other and give each other more space for the moment.

If jealousy is at the root of their issues, and the animals are having a hard time sharing their humans, it's important to talk to the animal about how their humans have more than enough love for everyone, and in fact it can increase with the presence of other animals. Their humans' feelings of love and joy increase from seeing them all get along and bonding. The animal can even be helpful to their humans if they work on being generous and welcoming with the other animals in the home. I would also make sure the animal knows how much their humans appreciate them working toward this goal, and how the harmony created by this process can also help the animal feel more at peace, safe, and happy in the long run. It can be very helpful to show the animal the bigger, long-term benefit to themselves that short-term harmony can eventually generate.

Animal communication used for behavioral challenges is often about compromising: What changes does the human need to make? Remember: It's not just about making the animals change. Often, we have to help our animals by changing things in the environment, including our own behaviors and habits.

What could be helpful tools to make everyone happy? Would more interactive play as a group be helpful, to help the animals create positive associations with each other? What about treat parties? Weekly catnip parties for the cats?

Training might be a good idea in a situation where animals aren't getting along, especially if it helps them work on their sense of boundaries and impulse control. Let's take the example of a dog who chases and barks at the other animals in their house in a way that isn't appreciated by the others. I would encourage the dog's human to work with a trainer and practice some safe-space training or boundary training. This is where you learn to call the dog over to their safe space (for example, their bed or mat), and have them stay there until they've been given the release word and are allowed to leave. Training like this could help the dog build self-control, which helps them learn to rein themselves in. It also encourages them to relax, even if they've been activated by a trigger, like another animal running by. If another animal in the home is being threatened by the one you're communicating with, you can also encourage that animal to give lots of space to the other one, so that everyone feels safe.

As always, you want to make sure the animals know what the long-term goal is: a home where everyone feels completely safe and confident, where they can lean on each other emotionally, and where they can see each other as friends and companions, playmates, and snuggle partners. You might even visualize what that could look like so you can be crystal clear with your communication. Would you like everyone to be able to lie on the same couch and share their space fully? Maybe you see them sharing the same bed together. In your vision, perhaps they are engaging in play together. Let your mind visualize the possibilities, and remember to let the animal know how grateful their humans are for the efforts they make toward that goal.

The following are two clients' experiences using animal communication for issues between multiple animals in the home or between animals and humans:

> We adopted a dog from our local shelter who was an
> unneutered two-year-old with an unknown background other
> than having been transferred from California to Oregon,
> where he was labeled a stray. He was on his best behavior
> for the first couple of weeks and we were perplexed by
> how anyone would let this perfect little guy go. But, as
> he settled in, we discovered his coping skills consisted of
> growling and biting, instead of the desire to willingly adapt.
> He claimed me as his friend and resisted my husband. Our
> cat fled under a bed and would only come out at night when
> the dog was safely kenneled. What had we done? We had
> turned our household upside down with this adoption and
> we were having a bit of "adopters' remorse." I turned to
> Thea for help. We felt her calm energy immediately as the
> dog lay near her while they communicated. After she let our
> dog share his perspective on the situation, Thea heard me
> out and conveyed information to our dog, explaining that
> my husband was part of the family and that it was important
> that we all get along. She communicated about the cat, too. I
> learned that our new dog's thought patterns were scattered,
> but he was trying to listen hard to us. He didn't know if he
> was supposed to submit to my husband or play with him. He
> hoped the cat would come out more often. The cat wanted
> some higher ground in the house before he would do so. I

can't relay it all, but what I tell people is that ever since Thea came to the house and communicated with both animals, our household has calmed down. Our dog and my husband are much cozier and the cat is venturing out more often. They're not "friends" yet, but I feel so much more optimistic since consulting Thea.

✦

We adopted a very anxious and troubled rescue dog, Kodi, and Thea helped us get a sense of his personality and what would make him feel more comfortable. For example, he appeared to have very severe separation anxiety. However, he communicated to Thea that he was okay with us going out for a while (though, of course, he would prefer that we never did!). He said it would help if we told him how long we would be gone, and after that, we always did, and still do! He's now much more comfortable with being left alone and takes it pretty much in stride.

Another time she helped us was when we adopted a puppy, and Kodi, three years old at the time, took an instant dislike to the pup and would not stop barking at him. We had a session with Thea scheduled, and she suggested to Kodi that the new puppy could be a fun friend, so he didn't need to bark at the puppy or feel threatened by him. After that session the incessant barking stopped completely.

More recently, after my husband passed away, a session with Thea helped to reassure me that Kodi was adjusting to the fact that my husband, whom he adored, was gone, and that he was happy living just with me. Kodi communicated through Thea that he would like to have something to challenge his brain (he's very smart) and Thea suggested food puzzles. I followed up on the suggestion and wow was she ever right! Kodi loves them, and he solves them so fast I can hardly keep up with him. Our communication sessions really helped us understand our mystery dog by letting us know what was important to him and vice versa.

Anxiety

Anxiety in an animal can come in so many different shapes and varieties, for so many different reasons. I will talk about separation anxiety and vet anxiety a little later, but I wanted to address general anxiety first. With an animal who is generally anxious, they tend to be on high alert for any threats in their environment. When I connect to an animal like this, it often feels like they are very sensitive to stimuli in their environment, and they have a hard time gauging what is actually dangerous and what isn't. For example, they might be worried about any and all sounds, especially if they can't see what caused them. They might jump any time your neighbor down the street slams their car door. They might be worried about inanimate objects. An unexpected slipper lying in a new spot might make them jump, or they might be too scared to walk by the trash can. They might be worried about certain people, or all people. They might be worried about certain animals, or all other animals.

Using animal communication can be helpful to identify what, specifically, the animal is anxious about: if it's just certain things that spark the anxiety, or if it's more of a generalized anxiety, and why they have that anxiety. What about the triggers feel scary to them? Did the anxiety come from traumatic events in their past? Or is it more of an issue of an overactive nervous system?

Does the animal need extra support with medications or supplements that target their anxiety? Would alternative therapies help support the animal's nervous system, such as acupuncture or massage therapy? Would training be helpful in this situation? I believe training is helpful in most situations involving anxiety, to help the animal potentially associate those triggers with positive things, such as treats or play. Training also helps give the animal a game plan for what to do or focus on when they see their trigger.

Using animal communication, we want to make sure we explain and reframe for the animal how their triggers are actually benign. We should also explain to the animal why they are safe in those triggering situations. For example, if sounds in the animal's environment trigger their anxiety, you should explain how those sounds are actually desirable in or outside the home because those are the sounds of life being lived, and that's a positive thing. You might explain to them what those sounds mean. When we hear shouting and running kids in the neighborhood, that means they're having fun. The banging sound we sometimes hear is just the neighbor taking out the trash. It can be helpful to explain to the animal that they can safely expect these big sounds or changes to happen in their environment every day, but that they are completely benign. That means it's safe for the animal to relax when they hear these sounds. It's safe for the animal to consider those sounds as background noise. Humans have great hearing, too, and often hear the same sounds and are not alarmed by them. If the animal is worried about a sound, you can encourage them to check in with their humans, and see if they are worried, too. If not, the animal can safely assume it's nothing to be alarmed about. When you communicate with an animal who is anxious about sounds, you can remind them that their humans have their safety under control.

I would use the same process of reframing to explain to the animal I'm communicating with if inanimate objects are the issue. I would emphasize that these objects—trash cans, misplaced slippers, etc.—are benign, or even helpful to have around us. If the issue is other animals, communication is a great opportunity to remind the anxious animal that we can trust that most humans or dogs we meet on our walks are safe, and even potential friends. You might share with the animal how happy it makes you to meet various neighbors and dogs, because you love to have new friends. You can ask your animal companion to help you make new friends by being a welcoming greeter.

What things about your own behavior or environment can you change to support your animal? With any of our animal companions who deal with anxiety, we have to make sure we are handling and working through our own anxiety as humans. If you get anxious about your animal's anxiety, that is, at the very least, not alleviating your animal's anxiety, and more likely it is contributing to it. Make sure you are supporting yourself in the ways you need to, in order to be grounded and centered and calm enough to support your animal through their anxiety.

If you have to bring your animal companion into a situation that you know will trigger their anxiety, I encourage you to take a few moments beforehand to get centered and communicate with them. Let's say your dog is anxious about other dogs on your walks and always gets very reactive. You should make sure that you are going on the walk with them in the best possible mindset. When people have a dog who is anxious on walks, they often begin dreading the walk long before they've even picked up the leash. When you're dreading something, anxious about what might happen, you're often replaying the worst-case scenarios in your mind, and it's likely that your dog is picking up on that.

The first thing you can do to help your dog release some of their anxiety about the walk before you step outside the door is to take a few moments to either meditate or sit quietly and get yourself into a space of calm relaxation. During that time, you can imagine what the ideal walk situation would be like. If you are having a hard time imagining it, try talking yourself through it. Maybe you envision a situation where your dog stays relaxed and calm, focusing only on you and the natural world around you, even if others walk by. Maybe your dog wags their tail when they see a stranger. Maybe the leash is fully slack while you two enjoy your walk together. You can direct your visualizations or thoughts to your dog and share with them that this is the goal. Let them know how grateful you are for their efforts to reach that goal. Then try to bring that calm, relaxed state with you as you walk out the door together. Walks are supposed to be a meditative bonding experience between animals and their humans, as well as about getting some fresh air and exercise. We want to make sure we get into that meditative, calm state ourselves, and help model that for the dog. You might be surprised how much your energy helps support your dog in feeling calmer and more relaxed.

If you've had some bad experiences with your dog on walks already, then it might take some effort, but it is very helpful to actively point out to your dog that the people or other dogs on your walks are potential friends. You want to model for your dog how wonderful you think it is to see others on your walks. Remind yourself and your dog that you love dogs, and love to make dog friends as much as possible, and how helpful it is if your dog is welcoming toward potential dog friends. You can remind them that you have safety under control on walks, that you will make sure to evaluate each situation as it comes up and decide if they're safe to enter or not. They can lean in to knowing that you will use your best judgment, and they can just relax.

Here is an example of a client of mine who was able to work through anxiety with her companion animal; this included altering her own behaviors:

I had experienced the passing of two beloved dogs over the past year, and had adopted two new dogs, so we were all going through major "growing pains." After I had a session with Thea, the details of those growing pains became more apparent to me, but I also had a number of potential solutions to work with. Because I was sure that I was still grieving over my deceased dogs, I made the decision to invite all four dogs into the session. That made for quite a circus, and I laughed and cried throughout the session! Thea did an amazing job of working to keep all of the conversations straight.

My newest rescue dog, Todd, was having some quite extreme and unexpected behavior challenges, and I was amazed at how Thea was able to work with him. I had had some maybe not-so-helpful animal communication sessions in the past, and wasn't aware that you could talk with an animal and explain how he could improve his behavior himself so that he could make things easier for us. I found it hilarious that Todd told Thea that he felt that he was "doing a great job" on walks, when he actually couldn't be within about a quarter-mile of people and other animals! Thea had excellent recommendations for him, as well as for me, as I was becoming quickly overwhelmed by his challenges.

We have since been working with a veterinarian behaviorist and a dog trainer, and things have improved greatly. I think the greatest help that Thea provided was a nudge for me: I realized that I also needed help for my own anxieties and insecurities related to Todd's challenges. I was also able to recognize and accept my ongoing issues with grief related to the passing of my two dogs over the past year, and get help for that as well. After the session, I listened to Thea's "Connecting to Your Passed Animals" meditation, and it changed my life again. I was able to easily feel the connection that I had with both of my previous dogs. The energy that I felt was palpable! I could never have imagined that I would still be able to feel the energies of my soul dogs, still so amazingly perfect in every way, although they were no longer with me. After that, I started learning animal communication myself. I was able to become a little more confident in my own abilities, and laugh at my "mistakes"! I found that I could have fun communicating with animals, both passed and present, in order to help others on their journeys as well. I'm so grateful to animal communication.

Separation Anxiety

Anxiety about being separate from their family can be really tough for animals. As domesticated pets, they have to adjust from their natural pack/flock/herd mindset to a very different way of living. Humans have busy lives, and even if we are lucky enough to be home with our animals most of the time, we still can't always bring our animal companions to the grocery store or to our doctor's appointments.

There's a spectrum of anxiety for each animal when it comes to being separate from their family. They are not always going to experience full-blown anxiety. Sometimes, they just feel loneliness. However, sometimes separation anxiety triggers severe physiological anxiety. Some pets even have a hard time when their humans are in a different room. As always, it's a good idea to ask the animal if they have a sense of why they have difficulty being separate from others. What about being separate is scary or triggering for them? What worries do they have when their humans are gone? For animals who are rescues or adopted from a shelter, some will have had traumatic experiences of being abandoned. If that's the case, it could be helpful to talk them through how that was a one-off event in their past, and how committed their current humans are, and how they will always come back.

For some, the sense of being in a pack or family is incredibly strong, and they feel unsafe when the pack isn't there around them at all times. It might be a good idea to explain to them how safe they really are, even when their family isn't around them. It also helps to communicate to the animal that in our society there are going to be situations in which their human has to go places where animals aren't allowed. Despite that, they are still all part of the pack, that the pack will temporarily separate but always comes back together. When their human goes out, they will always come back. I like to envision the family unit like a rubber band, especially when communicating with dogs. I show them how the modern pack is very flexible in our society, and that sometimes the pack expands out to the point where the different people and animals in the pack are in different places but they're still connected, and they always come back together, like a rubber band.

I also like to show an animal how they can use that alone time as downtime. If the animal tends to get very vocal, calling for their humans, I might explain to them how the crying/howling/barking doesn't help. For example, I may communicate to the animal that their owner is not actually near enough to hear them, and also point out that this vocalization just makes the animal more exhausted. I always encourage animals to rest and take care of themselves so that they have energy to have fun when their humans do come home. I might share with them how grateful their human would be if they tried to self-soothe. I emphasize how helpful it is to humans to know that their animal companion is home relaxing and safe. This discussion is all about shifting the animal's perspective so that they can value what they may have seen as distressing alone time as, instead, pleasurable downtime. That way, when their human leaves, the animal will see that their job is just to relax and take care of the home, and so there's nothing to worry about. Feeling that being relaxed is their responsibility can give them something to focus on and do that isn't searching for or calling for their humans.

For some animals, their anxiety is too overwhelming for them to even consider napping while their humans are gone. In most cases, you're going to need some sort of combination of animal communication and training or other tools to help the animal out. You might have to do a lot of training and practice leaving them for just a few seconds each time, then coming right back, before the animal gets to the point where they can tolerate being apart from you. You can use animal communication to get a sense of what tools and training might be most helpful. Does the animal feel that they need something to focus on while their humans are gone, like a distraction? Would they need something like a Kong filled with food or a puzzle toy, something to work on while their humans are away, so they have something positive to focus on? Would having another animal companion help the animal feel less alone? Do they need extra support with medications or supplements that alleviate anxiety? Is there a certain type of training they've tried that they feel would be helpful? What would be a good fit for their personality? Are they treat-motivated? Are they toy- or play-motivated? Crate training is often recommended for dogs. Would that be something the dog thinks is helpful? For some it would cause much worse anxiety if their biggest fear is being enclosed in a small space. For some it's necessary to remove access to anything they could damage by anxiety-chewing or harm themselves with. What other things could you give the animal to chew on that's not going to get damaged? Would working with a trainer be helpful, to give the animal a clear idea of what behaviors to do instead, and give them some positive reinforcement for those behaviors?

Again, you should make sure that you send your animal a clear idea of what the ultimate goal is: the point at which the animal will feel fully calm, quiet, and relaxed, snoozing or keeping herself occupied with toys, while her humans go out for a little bit. This should include sending them a clear image of their humans coming home each time as well, and the feeling of how grateful they will be for the effort the animal makes toward staying calm and relaxed.

If your own animal struggles with separation anxiety, remember that you can also connect to them yourself while you are away, simply by thinking of them and sending them reminders of when you'll be home as well as ideas for what they can do to keep themselves occupied in the meantime.

Here is an example of Danielle, a human whose dog Evelynn was suffering from separation anxiety before a communication session helped them both:

I had relocated to Portland from New York City, and my dog Evelynn, who always had a bit of separation anxiety, suddenly became incapable of being alone. She would scream and cry and scratch the doors from eight in the morning until noon when I was at work, loud enough that my neighbors left notes and I would come home to piles of paint shards in front of the door from her scratching. Even if my housemates and I went out to dinner, she would start crying before I even got my shoes on. I tried everything to soothe her: long walks beforehand, leaving the TV on while I was out, music, leaving treats out, etc. The only option I had left was medicating her, which I really didn't want to do. After a Google search, I came across Thea's website and decided to book a session. I figured I had nothing to lose. But once she arrived, I knew almost immediately I had made the right choice, because she connected first with my roommate's dog, who lives in the main house on the property (Evelynn and I lived in the detached studio). Thea described her manic energy perfectly and then commented that she seemed a bit smaller than Evelynn, which was true.

Once Thea connected with Evelynn, I was thrilled to hear all of my dog's thoughts. While Thea let me know she thought we were a great match and that Evelynn was happy (my heart melted, knowing that), Evelynn also made it clear that she wanted more treats, more walks, more ice cream, bigger windows to look out of, etc. It was exactly what I had expected Evelynn to vocalize! An absolute ham.

Without even having to tell Thea, she sensed that Evelynn was experiencing separation anxiety when I was out of the house. After I walked Thea through the situation, she started talking aloud to Evelynn, who was quite literally sitting at her feet and looking at her in the eyes for the entire pep talk. Thea reassured her that I would always come home, and that she should look at this alone time as a chance to relax, catch up on sleep, and enjoy having the bed and couch to herself. I remember Thea specifically told Evelynn to find a place in the apartment she found cozy and safe, such as the couch, and curl up there when she was feeling lonely.

I remember being home the rest of the weekend, but when I got ready for work on Monday, Evelynn was refreshingly calm. I tensed as I put on my shoes and grabbed my bag, waiting for the whining to start, but she jumped up on the couch and curled into the throw blankets. She watched me as I left, and for the first time in six months, I didn't hear her cry as I walked down the driveway. My housemates confirmed they hadn't heard her cry all day, and she hasn't cried since! Until I started working from home during the pandemic, she would curl into the same spot on the couch every morning as I left, just as Thea suggested. Now two years later, she greets me warmly and calmly every time I come home, and I can tell her stress has completely evaporated. It was a life-changing experience for both of us, and she's so happy! Especially when extra treats or ice cream is involved.

Sleep Disturbances

A paw scratching at your face in the middle of the night. Meows reverberating through the hallways at 2 a.m. The sudden sneak attack on your feet, startling you out of a deep sleep. The eager bouncing on you a good two hours before you're actually supposed to wake up. These behaviors can be endearing in their own way, but most of the time they are extremely annoying for humans. Unfortunately, these are also very common experiences if you live with an animal, and it's one of the behaviors that is incompatible with humans who like to get good, undisturbed sleep at night. Sleep is such an important thing for everyone, and getting our sleep schedules aligned with those of our animals is a big step toward creating harmony in the home. I've had a lot of clients schedule sessions with me solely based on their need to find a solution to their animal companion waking them up in the middle of the night.

There could be many reasons your animal companion is causing sleep disturbances. First, we have to remember that many animals have instincts that kick them into gear at dawn and dusk (some cats, for example). Additionally, many animals have learned to nap more during the day while their humans are busy with other things, which can then lead them to have a spike in energy around bedtime, and they take their boredom out on you. Nighttime disturbances may also be due to health issues, so, again, it is important to make sure the animal has seen a veterinarian. Additionally, older age can be a contributing factor to nighttime anxiety or confusion.

First up, when connecting to the animal, try to get a sense of why the animal is waking their humans/you up. Based on the animal's reasoning, see what compromises the humans could make in this situation, and what tools you could implement to alleviate the situation. If the animal has napped a lot during the day, their humans might need to help them adjust their schedule by being more active with them during the day or early evening before bedtime, to help them settle in for the night. If it's a cat who sleeps almost twenty hours a day anyway, then you might need to adjust their play and feeding schedule so that they play and eat closer to bedtime to help them sleep through the night.

After making note of what compromises and tools may be helpful for the situation, you should take a moment to clarify and explain to the animal what the humans are hoping for and why. I think it can help to explain to an animal that humans have sleep needs that are very different from theirs. They might be shocked to learn that humans need one longer, uninterrupted period of sleep each night to be happy and healthy. You can let the animal know that they can be most helpful to their humans if they stay calm or quiet during that time. Perhaps they are welcome to sleep with their humans or spend time in the same room if they can stay calm and quiet.

If they just naturally get a boost of energy at night, you can encourage them to go find other quiet activities, such as quiet toys to play with in a separate room, that won't be disturbing to the humans. In this situation, they might appreciate you keeping the window blinds on one window open for them to look out of at night.

If the animal is simply bored, impatient to be fed, or something else that isn't urgent, then we can ask the animal to please let their humans sleep until the humans decide it's time to get up. Most animals like to know when to expect that and like it to stay the same time every day. I once had a client whose two dogs were waking her up an hour or two earlier than she needed to. She requested that I ask them to please wait until 6 a.m. before waking her up. I explained the situation to them, including why their human was requesting this, but based on the dogs' collective excitement about mornings, I wasn't too hopeful that they would shift much. The day after our session, I received an email from the same client, who shared with me that her dogs had waited until 5:55 a.m. to wake her up, and, honestly, I was surprised they had waited that long!

Do animals understand time? I think it varies from animal to animal. Most seem to have a different sense of time than we do. Generally, in my experience they can understand concepts such as a period of daytime or nighttime. When you are trying to communicate something that might not be fully translatable (because animals don't live their lives by watches and clocks), they still can understand the gist of what you're saying, because the information is being translated for them in a way they can grasp. That's the benefit of communication that isn't limited by human language. So, for example, when you are telling your animal companion that you will be going to work and will be back in four hours, you aren't literally telling them "I'll be back in four hours"—you are sending them a feeling of how long that is. It's not short, like five minutes or even an hour, and it's not super long, like eight hours. Each amount of time you're trying to communicate comes with a feeling of its own that the animal can understand the gist of. I do think some animals have an excellent internal clock, even if they can't tell you exactly what time it is on the clock. Some certainly thrive on having a strict schedule, and will let you know when you're late to do something.

When communicating with an animal about wake-up times, I am sending them the *concept* of 6 a.m., and they are getting the gist of that concept as "early morning once it's started to get light outside." I also like to simply ask an animal to wait until their humans have shown signs of waking themselves up before they engage with them as they normally would. That way they have specific signs to look for that tell them it's okay to get the day started.

The reframing in this situation would be focused on showing the animal how much their efforts to stay calm and quiet at night really help their humans be much happier during the day. It also reminds the animal that if their human is able to rest all night, they'll have more energy to do other fun activities later. In addition, you should make sure to send the animal a vision of the ideal solution to this issue, where everyone is getting their needs met. Communicate a future in which the animal is calm, quiet, and relaxed throughout the night and morning, and if they are bored at night, that they go occupy themselves in a different room with quiet activities.

If an animal just has a case of restlessness, or just hasn't considered that humans need a different sleep schedule than they do, I have found most animals very amenable to suggestions about trying to let their humans sleep. Here's an example of a client who is a very light sleeper, and whose cat was waking her up at night, just from being the active cat that he is:

I contacted Thea to help me communicate with my dog and cat, but most especially my cat, Lenny. We got Lenny from the Humane Society at nine weeks old, and he was a wild child! Abandoned when he was just days old, he was bottle-fed and didn't really get the socialization and manners lessons a mama cat would have provided. So he played quite roughly, often drawing blood. He also frequently woke me up at night, which made me start closing my bedroom door and not letting him in. Lenny told Thea he was unhappy about being kept out of my room, and that he was lonely at night. She explained to him that I needed my sleep and told him if I kept the door open, he would need to promise not to wake me up. She asked if he could do that and he said he didn't think so. We proceeded with the rest of the reading, during which Thea explained that human skin is fragile and that he should try to remember to use "soft paws" when playing. Near the end of the reading, Lenny told Thea he had been thinking about it and decided he could indeed promise not to wake me up if I left my door open at night. I left the door open that night, and when I woke, he was sitting on the floor by the side of the bed quietly, and waited until I got up to wind around my feet and say good morning. He has never woken me up since, and waits for me every morning. And while he occasionally still plays rough, he rarely hurts anyone.

If the animal is older and experiencing cognitive decline and confusion, their internal clock might be off, causing them to wander at night. Some older animals seem to experience a spike in anxiety at nighttime as well. Nighttime can mean extra pain for some, either from lying down for longer periods of time, or when moving around during the day starts to catch up with them in the evenings. So they can get restless from the pain and have a hard time settling down. If it is a case of confusion or anxiety, it would be helpful to communicate to them that if they wake up and it's still completely dark around them (assuming they can still see a little bit), then they can trust that it is still nighttime, and they can safely lie down to rest and relax again. I might remind them that the more they can sleep during the night when it's dark, the better their body will feel during the day. If their nocturnal activity stems from pain, their humans should talk to the vet about managing that. Veterinary care for pain management can do a world of good for everyone's sleep and comfort.

Health Challenges

Going to the vet, taking medicine, and other issues related to health care can be a huge source of anxiety for your animals (and for you!). The next few sections outline some helpful scripts for making these scenarios more manageable—and even enjoyable—for you and your pet.

Vet Visits

Sometimes we have to do things with our animal companions that we know are unpleasant for them—things like vet visits or administering medications. I have a cat, Humphrey, who can be very fierce when he's feeling anxious and threatened. Years ago, I took him to the vet for a checkup, and he got so riled up and aggressive with the vets that they strongly hinted to me that Humphrey would be a good candidate for tranquilizers on future visits. Because he hadn't ever acted like that at the vet's before, I hadn't thought to use animal communication for him. So, before I brought him to his next visit to the vet, I made sure to do a few things differently, which helped him get through it more easily (and spared the vets a lot of stress).

1 Around a week before the appointment, I told Humphrey that I had scheduled a vet visit. Keeping secrets never works with pets. Secrets just confuse them, and can sometimes worry them more. When I told him about the upcoming visit, I got straight to the point and also told him why I was bringing him in. I explained to him when he could expect the vet visit to occur in terms of how many days or nights would pass before our appointment. I made sure to remind him a few more times over the next few days as well.

2 When I talked to Humphrey about the visit, I focused on the positive aspects: I emphasized that the vet is a safe place, that they will check his health and help him feel better, and that they love cats and that's why they do this work.

3 I focused on a vision of the ideal situation. I did not preface what I was saying with, "I know you hate the vet . . ." or "I know it was scary last time . . ." because when we do that, we're sending our animals the energy of those stressful feelings, reinforcing that in them. Instead, I focused on the best-case scenario, including a picture of what that would look like, and told Humphrey that the calmer and more relaxed we could be, the easier, quicker, and more pleasant

the visit would be. I told him that the more he could stay relaxed with the vet, the more he could help them help him.

4 Finally, I managed my own anxiety and worry. Any time I started to worry about the upcoming vet visit, I took a few deep breaths and released those feelings in order to make room for the ideal situation. I wanted Humphrey to know I was confident about the vet being safe and positive, and modeled that for him as best as I could.

The effect of this conversation was noticeable: Humphrey did amazingly well this time, without any tranquilizers, and even purred for a good portion of the visit. I was so proud of him!

I find it most helpful for people to be straightforward about their vet plans with their animal companions, keeping their carrier out for a few days beforehand before you go so they get used to seeing it and smelling it again, and then focusing on the positives of the upcoming visit. Also remember to visualize the goal of what a successful visit would look like ideally, where the animal fully relaxes into it, and even has a fun time seeing the people who care for their health. That way your animal companion can get a clearer idea of what a vet visit could potentially be, instead of picking up on our worries about worst-case scenarios.

Medications

When giving medications to an animal, you can use animal communication in the same way as in the scenario above. Basically, you want to let the animal know what to expect: in this case, the medication schedule (how often the animal will need to take medication, when and where, and for what duration). You'll also want to explain to the animal what the medications are for, and how the medications will positively affect them in the long run. Let them know that the more relaxed and calm they stay during the process, the easier it will be for everyone, and the more quickly it will be over.

You can also use your animal communication listening skills to see how the animal prefers to receive their medications, if they have any options. For example, do they prefer to get medication in a pill pocket, crushed and mixed with their food, or transdermally applied to the inner ear? Is the taste an issue, and if so, is there a way to mask that with something else? If it's an injection, is there a ritual that they like to have before or after the injection, like a session of snuggling, or do they prefer to get the injection over with without a lot of preamble? Do they prefer to be distracted while you give the medication? Would they like to approach the event of being medicated more like a training session, where they get rewarded afterward if they do a good job?

My cat companion Gilly has asthma, so she needs to receive her asthma medications with an inhaler, along with a mask that fits her face. Since Gilly is not the type to allow anyone to do just anything with her, and she hates being restrained and feeling like she can't escape, I decided to train her with treats to use the inhaler and mask. She's super smart, and very food-motivated, so that strategy was a good fit for her personality. I have used my communication skills with her to explain what we're doing, why we're doing it, how the inhaler really helps her, and what she can do to make the process more effective and helpful. Now she is sure to let me know when it's time to give her the inhaler.

Tuning in to Health Issues

Another practical way to use animal communication is by getting a sense of how an animal is feeling in their body: whether they have pain or other physical ailments, and how they want that handled. Taking care of an animal's health can be very stressful, because so often trying to figure out what's wrong with an animal's health is like a guessing game with high veterinarian bills. Animal communication can be a useful tool in combination with the veterinarian—communication can help you to gain clarity on what medical interventions would be most useful, or whether they're making the animal feel better. So often we're not aware of the aches and pains going on in our animals, as they can be very good at hiding certain issues. Animal communication may be helpful in getting ahead of potential health challenges so that we can bring the animal in to the vet earlier, before their health gets worse.

One great technique to get a better sense of an animal's body and how they are feeling physically is by merging energy fields with the animal, as we noted in an earlier chapter. The process is similar: After you've connected heart to heart with the animal, ask them if you can merge your energy fields together to assess their physical health. Visualize yourself surrounded by a bubble of light, and visualize the animal surrounded by their own bubble of light, and then visualize these two bubbles of light merging together so that you are both in the same bubble and sharing energy fields. As you experience what it feels like to be in the animal's body, you might notice a sense of subtle pain in certain areas of "your" body, or notice other things that seem odd.

Another technique for determining what might be going on with an animal's health is to scan their body. This is more of a psychic technique, where you are simply tuning in to the animal's energy field, instead of getting the information in a conversation with the animal. You are taking the initiative to scan their energy field, so you might even feel things that they themselves are not fully aware of. But, again, this isn't like taking an X-ray. It's still an intuitive technique, which requires interpretation, so it's not a technique that can be used to diagnose or rule out health issues. However, it might provide some extra insights that could help you out when communicating with a veterinarian.

To do this technique, you would first take a moment to get still and centered, getting into a receptive state of awareness. Then, if you are in person with the animal, you would use your eyes (or your hand hovering over the animal's body) and scan from the animal's head to their tail, noticing where your awareness is drawn to on or in their body. You might feel your eyes or hand pulled to a certain spot, or notice what spots on the animal's body "look" energetically different to you. You might feel some spots are "warmer" or "colder" than others, or you just might get a *knowing* about a certain area having difficulties. You might hear a word or two in your mind about which areas are having issues, like *leg* or *heart*. If you are not physically near the animal, you can do the same thing. First, imagine the animal in front of you, and then imagine scanning them from head to tail. You could even merge energy fields with the animal as in the technique above, scanning *your* own body as a way to scan *their* body. Notice where your awareness is being drawn to.

Health is a topic that comes with a great deal of pressure, making it a fertile opportunity for the brain to jump in with unwanted random guesses as to what's wrong. With high pressure and complicated topics like health, it's best to make sure you slow down and take baby steps, resisting the urge to try to see the big picture all at once. Health situations tend to be much more complicated than they initially appear, and yet our brain has a tendency to want to simplify things. Our brain wants to jump to conclusions and see the full picture immediately. It wants to go into diagnosing mode. Our challenge with high-pressure topics like this is to keep our spastic brains out of the picture as much as possible during a session. We do that by slowing down, taking it baby step by baby step, and seeing things more like individual puzzle pieces from the animal that could eventually lead to a full picture of their health situation. There might be many facets to what is really going on, and our job is only to acknowledge the individual impressions we're receiving, even if we're not quite sure how they might combine and lead us to the root cause of our animal's discomfort. We need to resist the urge to make assumptions based on the first few pieces of information we receive.

In general, I don't recommend relying too much on animal communication for the diagnosis and treatment of an animal, especially if it's your own animal companion that you're connecting to. Since animal communication is not a perfect science, it's *always* a good idea to bring your pet to a veterinarian as the first course of action. You could then potentially hire a separate animal communicator as support to go deeper if the vet isn't quite sure what's going on. Determining health issues in our own animal companion is fraught because we're always going to have some bias due to our emotional connection to the animal. That's the same reason doctors are discouraged from treating or operating on their own family members. If you want support to get clarity on a pet's health situation, in addition to working with a vet, it might be worth hiring an animal communicator who is not personally connected to your animal.

Animal communication should never be a substitute for veterinary care, but it can be a helpful complement to it. In an ideal world, we would all have access to each discipline and be able to use both. Veterinary care can pick up on things that animal communication misses, and animal communication can pick up on things that veterinary care misses. A little while ago I had a client whose dog had been exhibiting some new aggressive behaviors, such as ferociously growling any time anyone came near. Before our appointment, she brought her dog to the vet to see what might be wrong. The vet pressed on the dog's body to test for any pain responses, but the animal didn't react, so the vet sent the dog home, saying it was likely an anxiety or behavioral issue, and not a result of pain.

However, during my session with the dog, he shared with me that he had been having quite a bit of pain in his hips and lower back. He also shared with me that he had been protecting his body so that it wouldn't hurt more. When the client shared her recent experience at the vet's with me, I was surprised that the doctor hadn't seen anything that would indicate body pain. I made sure to check in with the dog about the aggressive behavior, to see if there was possibly a different reason for it, but the dog insisted he was just trying to protect himself from more pain. I let the client know what her dog was showing me and encouraged her to check with the vet again if she could. I also made sure to talk the dog through the aggressive behavior, just in case I was misinterpreting something—in case it was due to anxiety, even if I personally didn't think his behavior would change until he got the pain addressed.

After our session, the client scheduled another appointment with the vet and insisted on getting an X-ray of her dog's hips. That's when the vet found severe hip dysplasia in both hips, as well as arthritis in his joints. After getting appropriate medications for her dog's pain, the client checked in with me a few months later to give me an update. She told me that her beloved dog was now back to his bouncy old self, and that he was no longer growling at others or aggressively protecting his body. This is just one example of how animal communication can support veterinary care.

Other times, the information an animal shares in a session is just for their human's information, and not always something that can be solved by a veterinarian. Health issues may have already progressed without anyone, including the animal, having been aware of them until it was too late. The following is a client's experience with her dog, who had seemingly recovered from cancer at the time of our appointment, but whose communication session became a beautiful memory to have after her dog's passing not long after:

> Thea helped me to understand my dog Mellie better, while she was still alive. In my session with Thea and Mellie, we talked about many things, such as Mellie's likes and dislikes, her habits, as well as Mellie's suggestions for my relationships. Thea also went into how Mellie was feeling physically. Thea mentioned that Mellie, who had just recovered from cancer, had some new discomfort in her bladder area. A few weeks later I took her to her oncologist and they let me know that the cancer was back and in her bladder. I was in awe. Our session made the last two months we shared together incredibly special. I cherish the memory of that day.

✦

CHAPTER 4

Aging and Dying Animals

Working with aging and dying animals is not just helpful for the animals, but also for their humans. When an animal is ill or elderly, it's normal for us to become hyperaware of their mortality, and we can start to dread the day we have to say goodbye to our beloved companions. This is a stage of the relationship where often the human has already started their grieving process, even before the animal has passed. Animal communication can be helpful in providing some support for both parties, and can offer some guiding information to help everyone prepare for the animal's last months in their body.

There are many topics you can go into with an animal that is at the end stage of life. Most notably, how they're feeling in their body and what they would like done to help them feel better. What their wishes are for their passing and what they would like to do before they cross over. This is also an opportunity for the animal and their human to reminisce about the life they've had together, as well as create meaningful rituals that can bring a sense of closure and peace between them as the animal gets ready to release their body.

Important Topics When Connecting to Severely Ill, Old, or Dying Animals

✦ Symptoms they've been having or their most important issues of discomfort. What are their pain levels on a scale from 1 to 10? Are current pain medications helping, or do they want more support?

✦ Do they have wishes regarding medications and treatments?

✦ Do they have a bucket list? Things they'd like to do, people or animals they want to see, places they want to go, if possible?

✦ What are the animal's preferences for passing? Euthanasia or on their body's own time?

✦ If the animal prefers euthanasia, what kind of farewell ceremony would they like? Who would they like present for the euthanasia (including other pets, other humans, etc.)? Where do they want it done? At home? Indoors or outdoors? Do they have a favorite spot?

✦ Do they have suggestions for what signs to look out for when it might be the right time for them to pass?

✦ What are some of their favorite memories together?

✦ Is there anything else they would like their humans to do for them before they pass?

Some people want to know when their animal will pass. This, I think, is our attempt to find some certainty in a phase of life that is rife with uncertainty. However, I don't know if it is the most useful question to ask. Getting a sense of when the animal will pass is tricky. Sometimes the animal does have a good sense of it, and sometimes they don't. Sometimes it's just a complete guess on both the animal communicator's and the animal's part. Also, I think we should ask ourselves, would it be helpful if we knew when the animal might pass? Let's say we make a prediction like that, and then we're wrong. The human will have wasted a lot of energy being anxious about that time for no reason.

I do think it's helpful to get a sense of where the animal is at mentally and physically with regards to their health and potential future passing. Do they still have a strong will to live? Are they still chugging along? Or are they preparing themselves to cross over soon? Do they feel more hopeless about their situation? And is this based in facts of their health, or is it more due to an underlying depression they're experiencing due to their situation? Are they still experiencing joy and pleasure from their life, and are those joys still outweighing the discomfort of their declining health? Once you get a sense of the animal's current state of mind and energy levels, you can then dive into their desires for continuing treatments, medications, care, and anything that could improve their situation.

Is it okay to ask an animal how they would like to transition, even if the timing of their death isn't necessarily right away, but just on the horizon, due to older age? Yes, absolutely. Animals don't take offense to that sort of question, and they are very aware of death and the spirit world already. However, if you are connecting to someone else's animal, be sure to recognize that their human might not feel ready for that topic yet, in which case we should be respectful.

If you are in the situation where your animal companion is close to passing, whether with help through euthanasia or on their body's own time, here are some things you can do to make it the best experience possible for everyone involved:

✦ Be present with them.

✦ Communicate with them about what's going on and why.

✦ Communicate how much you love and appreciate them.

✦ Reminisce out loud about all the good times you've had together.

✦ Try to keep the energy uplifted and loving and calm, if you're able to. Helpful ways to do that might be thinking about the wonderful things you've gotten to do together, and the wonderful things they'll get to do on the other side when they pass away. It's also 100 percent okay if you're doing this all through tears and heartbreak.

✦ Engage in their favorite activities with them, if possible, before they pass.

✦ Give them their favorite treats and foods before they pass.

✦ Bring them to their favorite spot, if it can be done so they're still comfortable.

What each animal wants will always be specific to them as an individual, so if we are able to give them the gift of listening, we can help them have the best experience possible at the end of their time with us. Think of this as an opportunity to help them have a little more joy and a little more ease before they go. And know that they hear and understand what you're trying to tell them.

The following is a story about a client of mine I was able to help at the time of her cat's passing:

Thea helped my husband and me with connecting to our dying indoor cat Lilly. She was having health issues at fifteen years old. Thea helped me to hear what Lilly wanted me to know. I wanted Lilly to let me take care of her and keep her comfortable. But, instead, she kept walking away from me, and I often couldn't find her in the house. She would hide. In our session with Thea, Lilly let me know that what she wanted was to be by herself. I got it and did what I could for her, and the night she actually died, she came close to our bed in the middle of the night and she let me put her in the middle of the bed with us and she died before sunrise. I felt her love and was grateful that she came to me and allowed me to comfort her. Although, in the end, I know that what she was doing was comforting me.

✦

CHAPTER 5

Wild Animals

I am sure all of us would love to snuggle up with a fox friend, or have a beautiful experience with a wild wolf who has somehow decided to become our companion. Who wouldn't feel massively honored by that? However, when it comes to animal communication with wild animals, we need to be just as realistic with our expectations as we are with domesticated pets. Just because wild animals can potentially hear and feel you communicate with them does not mean that they will respond, react, or even want to connect with you. In fact, in most cases, wild animals have much less reason to listen to a human than a domesticated animal does. There are a few things that can stand in the way of a successful conversation, namely: They might strongly distrust or fear you as a human, or they might view you as truly insignificant to them. They typically have no emotional bond with you or any other human you might speak for. A wild animal is unlikely to have much incentive to connect with or listen to you.

In a few cases, a wild animal might have more reason to connect: When they have to deal with humans more, and when it would benefit them to be part of a conversation. For example, communication with wild animals

Exercise: Connecting to Wild Animals

If you would like to work more closely with wildlife, I recommend spending more time amongst them. You can go for a walk in nature and sit down somewhere comfortable. You might try meditating or focusing on your breath. If you can work on calming your own energy, the wildlife around you will likely respond with trust. Note that staying at a respectful physical distance from wild animals also tends to build trust.

Then try reaching out to the wildlife you notice around you. Practice the steps of connecting, asking for permission to communicate, sending lots of love, awe, and humility, and introducing yourself. Make sure to let them know what your intentions are for connecting. Are you hoping to help them in some way? Do you want to ask them a favor? Do you want to learn from them? Do you simply wish to be in communion with them? Release your expectations of a certain response from them, and also release your need for proof of your communication. See this as an exercise in loving presence, and open listening to what they are willing to share. And when you're done communicating, make sure you give your heartfelt thanks.

can be very useful when working with a wild animal rescue organization or a wildlife rehabilitator. The same is true when working with animals who are wreaking havoc; or animals who pose a danger to others, such as squirrels burrowing under people's houses causing damage; or animals in danger of being killed by pest-removal services. We can also reach out when we are sharing space together with wild animals, in their natural habitats, and open channels of communication. Some wild animals will also be more curious and want to connect for fun, and some might have messages to share. It's not only domesticated animals who live with humans who carry deep wisdom. Wild animals accumulate wisdom throughout their lives, from their own experiences, just as other animals do. I do think there's a tendency for animals in general to be much more spiritually attuned and aware. So, if you approach a wild animal in the right way, they might be open to sharing their wisdom with you.

Connecting with wild animals is similar to connecting with domesticated animals, in that the process is the same. The difference is in our intentions and how we approach the wild animals. First and foremost, I think we need to view our connection with wild animals with humility, even more so than we do with our animal companions. We are encroaching on their energy, their time, and often their territory. We want to be respectful and honor their needs, just as we do with other animals. We want to make sure that we ask them for permission to communicate, sending lots of love and respect to them. It's also important for us to share with them our reason for connecting. Are you hoping to help them in some way? Do you want to ask them for a favor? Do you simply wish to be in communion with them? Make sure they know your motivation when you initially reach out. And when you're done communicating, always give them your heartfelt thanks.

Earlier this year, someone in my town reached out to me via email, describing to me a recent run-in with a skunk. Said skunk had somehow gotten a large rat trap caught on their front paw. This person was trying to catch the skunk using a humane trap, so that she could bring them to a vet or otherwise help them remove the trap. This was all a big ordeal, and she was contacting me to see if I could help it go more smoothly by communicating with the skunk. Although she wanted to help the animal, she really didn't want the skunk to scratch or spray her (understandably). She sent me a photo of the skunk, so I connected to the skunk as I normally would, introducing myself, sending feelings of awe, love, and humility, asking if I could communicate. I also let them know why I was connecting.

I shared the woman's plan with the skunk, about wanting to help remove the rat trap so they could be more comfortable. I showed the skunk that they could trust that the lady wanted them to feel better again, and that the humane trap was set up for her to do that. I encouraged the skunk to go into the trap and stay as calm and relaxed as possible so that the lady could help remove the rat trap. Additionally, I shared that the plan was to ultimately release them back to their family.

At the same time, I sent the skunk lots of imagery of what the ideal situation would be: of the skunk walking into the humane trap, staying calm and relaxed inside, maybe taking a nap and feeling safe and loved while humans helped them. I didn't say, "Don't scratch or spray" at all, because I didn't want to send mixed signals. I just focused on sharing the message about staying calm and relaxed, and the idea that the animal could even focus on taking a nap while they were safe inside the humane trap. If they could be as gentle and relaxed as possible, then the human would be done much more quickly. I also coached the woman who had contacted me through how she could communicate the same things to the skunk.

A few days later the same lady got back to me with an update. She had managed to trap the skunk.

> The little guy was a perfect angel. Very calm, continued to eat while in the car, and I think took a nap coming home. When removing the trap, not a peep or squeal . . . just a moment of "That feels different."

I have also had the honor of communicating with deceased wild animals who lived at an animal sanctuary. A few years ago, while putting my daughter to bed, I was sitting on her bed in the dark when I suddenly felt the familiar feeling of a spirit connecting to me, and, in my mind's eye, I saw a big wild cat. It wasn't a crystal-clear image, but it did look something like a tiger, or some other big cat. Along with this image, I got the sense that the animal was coming to let me know that it would be working with me some time in the near future. It was so random and unexpected that I didn't take it too seriously; nonetheless, I filed it away in the back of my mind.

About a month later, I was doing a reading for a client, and in this reading, after connecting to several of her dogs, both deceased and living, I felt some much larger presences step into my energy field, calling for my attention. With one of them I got an overwhelming sense of being looked down upon, as if this creature were by far my superior in every way. I described to my client the impressions I was getting, including the visual impressions, size, and personality, and asked her if this made sense in terms of the animals connected to her. I personally was still not expecting an actual big wild cat to connect in a session, but she let me know that she knew exactly who I was talking to: two tigers and a black leopard she had worked with through a wild animal sanctuary and rescue. The tigers and leopard shared that they had messages for both my client and a few others who had worked with him, including the woman who was his caretaker and ran the sanctuary where he had lived.

The leopard, in particular, wanted most of all to acknowledge the positive work his caretaker was doing by helping rescue animals like him. He shared with me how he had been confined to an incredibly small space before he came to her sanctuary. Turns out he had been kept in a tiny cage for most of his life. He then wanted to share how grateful he was for the larger space he got to have at her sanctuary. This was a poignant message for her because she had been racked with guilt over not being able to offer him a much larger enclosure than she had (ideally, she had wanted to offer him something closer to the range a black leopard would normally have in the wild). The leopard saw the habitat he got at her place as a massive improvement over the tiny cage he had been kept in before being rescued. He encouraged her to continue her work so that she could keep helping others like him who were harmed or let down by humans in their past.

Before the leopard left our session, he made sure to share a bit about some of the things he loved and hated in life. He showed me how he loved to stalk the humans who came to visit the sanctuary, from inside his enclosure. The deep humor and joy he got out of that was a wild experience for me, as I am not used to feeling quite so much enjoyment out of wanting to hunt and kill other animals, much less other humans. I will let my client share more in her own words about her experience here:

I had reached out to Thea to do a combo reading—one for my three dogs, most especially my little rescued and disabled pit bull, Rita—and the other to connect with wild animals from an animal rescue foundation I had worked with, who had recently passed. We started with a reading for my dogs, and many questions were answered. I had worried about how my ten-year-old lab, Leonard, was processing the recent death of his best friend Tom. What Thea shared about Leonard's feelings confirmed what I knew to be true, based on the details she gave me. It was a huge healing for all of us, but most especially Leonard. The funniest thing about that portion of the reading was how Rita, our disabled pit bull, kept talking over the other dogs. She kept bringing the conversation back to her, like how much she loved her toys. We had to ask her to please let the other dogs speak!

When we got to the portion of the session in which Thea would be communicating with the wild animals who had lived at the rescue foundation, I was in shock at how much detail Thea gave. Two tigers I had worked with closely came through, and I knew with 100 percent certainty because the tigers mentioned private details that only people with a close relationship to the founder of the sanctuary would know. Thea shared the strength of the tigers' love for the founder and some of the special things she did for them. These details aren't publicized and wouldn't have been known by anyone who wasn't close to the founder. What was really wonderful was that I had only wanted to talk to the tigers, but other animals came through as if sensing they had an opportunity to share messages that I could give to the founder of the wildlife rescue. They let her know how much they loved her and confirmed that the special things she did meant a lot to them.

One unexpected guest was Mateo, a regal black leopard who had recently passed away at the age of twenty. Mateo was a very serious leopard who didn't connect with many people when he was alive. In fact, he wasn't very sociable at all, so it was a shock to have him come through and speak to Thea. Thea immediately and correctly sensed his very strong, powerful energy. Details about his personality—like how he loved stalking people!—his medical issues, and his love of his enclosure were all correct. We even had a laugh as Mateo was a bit of a snob—he let Thea know she was just a simple human trying to translate! While I couldn't confirm some of the details Mateo shared during the reading, I was able to speak to the founder of the rescue later, and she verified everything. The communication from Mateo and the tigers was a delightful surprise, and so healing for all of us who had worked with them.

✦

PART THREE

Spiritual Beings

CHAPTER 6

Passed Animals

Mediumship is what we call the art of communicating with the spirit world. Typically, you will hear the word *mediumship* in reference to communication with passed human loved ones. However, speaking with passed animals follows the same process. It functions the same way, and both animals and humans are all in the same "space" in the spirit world. There is no "animal heaven" that is separate from "human heaven." They are both in the same "heaven," and are able to mingle freely. This is why, when you do a session connecting to an animal who has passed, you might have human loved ones who have passed join the conversation, and vice versa.

Communication with animals who have passed away is very similar to connecting to animals who are still living. In both cases, you are connecting soul to soul with an animal. In the case of an animal who has passed, the difference is, of course, that they no longer have a body. There are also differences in the types of information that might come through from the animal, such as how they passed and any messages they have for their human on that topic.

The other side is not above us, nor is it below us. It is all around us. And since we are spirits inhabiting physical bodies, we are already a part of the spirit world while also part of the physical world. We have both feet in both worlds at the same time, and both worlds are completely intertwined. And just as when we are connecting to animals still living, we don't need any big ritual to connect to the other side. The process of connecting is simply a shift in perception, of placing your awareness on the spirit world.

Even if the spirit world is not above us, many do still find it helpful to direct their awareness to a spot a little bit above their head when connecting to the other side. Whatever your awareness is on, that's where you're connecting. When communicating with a living animal, that is very much an outward connection: You project messages, impressions, and emotions horizontally from your heart to connect to the animal's heart. But when communicating with an animal on the other side, we can place our awareness a bit above us to connect to the animal there. This helps set our intention for who and what we wish to connect to, and to clarify that we are not trying to connect to an animal in the living world, but rather are hoping to connect to one in the spirit world. There are different ways you can do this as well. Lately I have been finding it useful to envision that I am opening up a gate to the spirit world above me. I mentally invite my client's deceased animal companions into the session that way. Some envision a space like a beautiful garden and invite the animal's soul to meet them there in that vision.

Just as when we are connecting with other humans, it helps to be respectful, loving, and open-minded when you ask an animal's spirit to connect to you. The other side is full of love, understanding, and joy, and oftentimes it helps if we can embody that energy ourselves in the reading, to strengthen our connection. Mediumship is, in a sense, about frequency. The spirit world vibrates at a certain frequency, and we living humans vibrate at a different frequency. For the two of us to connect, we must raise our frequency, and they must lower theirs, so we meet in the middle. One way of doing that is by placing our daily issues to the side and focusing on lifting our energy and mood to prepare for our session. Then we must intentionally place our awareness on the spirit world and on the spirits we intend to connect to.

Some people worry that when mediums connect to passed animals or humans, we are somehow disturbing them or forcing them to show up in some way. It's important to note that we actually have no control over those on the other side, including animal souls. Being able to control those on the other side would indeed make my job a heck of a lot easier, but alas that is not within my power. If we ask the spirits of animals who have passed to come through in a session, they will usually show up because they want to connect to their humans again. However, we can no more summon someone from the other side than we can summon a living person in the physical world. We can only ask, and they choose whether or not to show up. In most cases, they do so because of the bond of love they have with their human.

Evidence in Animal Mediumship

What kind of information normally comes through in a reading with an animal who has passed? Usually, a lot of the same things as with an animal who is living, but with some added topics and additional focus on healing messages for their humans.

✦ Personality

✦ Physical appearance

✦ Mannerisms

✦ Their family relations (any other animals they lived with, any human family members, information about who they bonded with most and how they felt about the other animals at home, etc.)

✦ Habits (good or bad)

✦ Behavioral challenges they had in life

✦ Interests, likes/dislikes, any favorite toys/activities/foods

✦ Favorite memories they had with their humans

✦ Their home environment

✦ Their greater role in their human's life

✦ How they passed (quickly, slowly, as a result of a disease, by means of euthanasia, of old age, by an accident, etc.; if from a disease, what disease or what part of the body was affected)

✦ If euthanasia, what were the surrounding circumstances contributing to that decision

✦ If they were ill, all the ways their human helped them through their illness (treatments, or reasons why treatments weren't done)

✦ The ways they've been commemorated by their humans

✦ Who they are with on the other side

✦ What they are up to on the other side

✦ What their plans are regarding reincarnation (if they have decided to reincarnate, or if they will wait on the other side to greet their human when they pass)

✦ Signs they send their humans to show they are still around them

✦ Things they have witnessed happening in their family's life since they passed, to confirm they have been with them during that time

✦ Messages for their humans (love, forgiveness, understanding, guidance, etc.)

If you are doing a reading for someone else, generally you will want to follow where the spirit wants to go in the conversation, and allow them to tell you their story. If you are searching for only specific types of information from them, you are attempting to control the conversation, which can end up halting the flow of energy, and your logical thinking brain will likely start to get in the way.

The evidence that comes through in an animal mediumship reading can be an important healing aspect of the reading, because it shows how the animal truly still is around, despite not having a physical body anymore. Just that knowledge can give so much peace. Here is the experience of a couple who sought out my services, to try to find some relief from the grief they were experiencing after the loss of one of their dogs, Dante:

A few years ago, my husband and I lost our beloved dog, Dante, after a few months of his brave battle against nasal cancer. The grief from losing Dante was overwhelming, unbearable at times, so I decided to research animal mediums on the internet. I believe it was fate that led me to Thea. After researching Thea's website, I decided to schedule a mediumship reading of Dante and an animal communication session with our living dog, Dora. On the day of the session, we sat on the other side of the country, connected to Thea via Skype, as she began receiving information. Having no prior knowledge of our pups other than their pictures and names, Thea began relaying information first from Dante. We were instantly amazed at the accuracy of detailed information that flowed from Dante to Thea; his illness, times shared during family outings, Dante's relationship with Dora, all this and more, which confirmed to us that Dante's funny and beautiful spirit communicated with Thea and that his spirit lives on, actively interacting with and aware of all our goings-on.

What followed the reading with Dante was just as amazing and astonishing to us—the reading with Dora. Dora had been sitting a few feet away from us when Thea was providing the messages from Dante. As Thea started to telepathically "tune in to" Dora, we noticed that Dora sat up as if someone had called her name. She sat silently but had quite a perplexed look on her face. Thea relayed information from Dora, first to confirm that it was, in fact, Dora she was connected to and she was not still receiving information from Dante. Due to our strong bonds with Dante and Dora, knowing their unique personalities, we were able to verify to Thea that she was now communicating with Dora. Thea relayed specific information related to Dora's health and her personality, details about the people Dora and my husband encountered in their daily walks at the park, and issues, like coming when we call her, which Dora says she is working on to improve. This message provides me with comfort to this day and is one that I still cling to for comfort . . . that Dora still feels Dante around her, lying together as they always had.

Evidence After Their Passing

One of the most powerful parts of a reading with passed animals is often in the evidence about how they are still around their humans, even if they no longer have a body and aren't physically present. There are multiple things they might bring up to show this. They might mention the ways they've been commemorated by their humans since their passing: for example, things that were done with their remains, ceremonies that were performed, special objects that were created, pictures that were put up, tattoos that were gotten, letters that were written, candles that were lit, trips that were taken, conversations that were had—all in memory of them. They might bring up the signs they've sent their humans to show they are still around (signs they have already sent, and signs they have yet to send). They might focus on situations that have come up in their human's life since their passing, to show that they've been present and are still involved in their human's life, despite not being there physically.

First, this shows that the animal is still around, and that the medium is not just connecting to some kind of memory of the animal—they are connecting to the actual soul that still interacts with their human. Second, it may also be a stepping-stone to encouraging the human to reach out to their animal themselves and continue their personal connection, showing them that they don't need a medium to connect them to their animal companions.

I had a reading with a client a few years ago who had just lost her dog. During our session, this dog came through and told his human that he would connect to her and send her a sign through her friend who was also into mediumship. The client wasn't entirely sure about this or how this would happen, but I let her know to keep it in mind, because her dog was quite insistent on this. A few days after our reading, the client was listening to the recording of our session on her own, and she got to the part where I was relaying the message from her dog that he would connect through her friend. Just then, her phone rang, from said friend, and when she picked up, there was no one on the line. Apparently her friend's phone had called her, at that exact moment, without her friend's knowledge. This was her beloved dog's way of showing her that he truly was around her.

Other important topics that the animal might bring up include what they are up to on the other side, who they are with there, and who came to greet them when they passed. This might be people and animals the animal knew in life who came to greet them when they passed, or it could also have been humans and animals they didn't know in life, but that were somehow connected to their own human. So if the client's mom passed long before the client's horse passed, the mom might still have shown up and greeted the horse once he passed away, because the mom cares about her daughter, and, by extension, she cares about her daughter's animal companions.

The question of what the animal is up to on the other side is one of those that varies from animal to animal. I've had animal souls reference taking on a role as spirit guide for their human, meaning that they play an active part in helping them out from the other side, with different areas of their life. I've had animal souls reference doing things they weren't able to do in life, such as eat whatever they want, play, spend all their time at the beach, or continue their favorite activities on the other side. I've had animal souls reference doing bigger-picture jobs like helping other animals cross over, or bringing healing to souls living or passed. There are many things that could occupy a soul once they cross over, and it can be a fascinating topic if they choose to share what they've been up to.

Reincarnation

The question of reincarnation comes up quite a bit in animal mediumship sessions, both from clients and from animal souls. This is actually a bit of a controversial topic. Not all of us mediums and animal communicators agree about reincarnation. This is probably because the universe is so vast, and we can't possibly fathom the whole truth behind how everything works on the other side, especially regarding technicalities of the soul, birth, rebirth, past lives, and how it's all possible. On this topic, along with all other topics in this book, I believe it's important to allow the individual animal souls to show you what is true for them.

Some animal souls have shown me their plans to reincarnate fully, to come back to their humans in a different body, although in my experience this happens less often than one might think. Most animal souls have shown me that they are not planning on reincarnating anytime soon, and would rather wait for their humans on the other side. And yet other animal souls have shown me their plans of partial reincarnation, meaning part of their soul reincarnates into a different body, while most of their soul or higher self still remains on the other side. To be completely honest, I truly have no clue how any of this is possible. But if we keep our minds open, that allows the individual animal souls to explain what is true for them.

In either case, it's important for people to understand that there could be a myriad of reasons an animal chooses a particular path. I know that for many people it can come across the wrong way if an animal chooses not to reincarnate back into their human's life. That might make us think that, since the animal chose not to reincarnate, they don't think their humans were good companions or caretakers for them. In my experience, if an animal chooses not to reincarnate, it's often because they feel like they can currently be of more use to their humans by helping them from the other side (especially if they are taking on the role of spirit guide for them). Or, the animal might have another important job to do on the other side for a while. Perhaps they want to be sure that they are the first ones to greet their humans when their humans cross over eventually. Perhaps they have plans to send other living animals to their human, animals who need their human's help or animals who are going to be instrumental in their human's life.

It is absolutely not personal if your beloved animal companion decides to stick to the other side for now. As I mentioned, in my experience this is often what an animal chooses to do when they pass. However, here and there I have sessions with animals who choose to reincarnate, which is always an interesting, fun surprise. Here is one client's experience:

> I lost my beloved dog, Opal, after she was attacked and killed by another dog. It was such a devastating ending to the absolutely epic friendship we shared. I had never felt that level of grief in my life. I had absolutely no idea how I could live without her. I spent weeks trying to figure out who I even was now, if I wasn't her mama. My husband's worry about me grew as my sadness continued, and he thought it might be time for me to get some help. I knew traditional counseling wouldn't even come close to what my heart needed. I decided the only thing I needed to know is that she was okay. I started looking into and researching mediumship. During my reading, I was not only able to find out that Opal was indeed okay, but that she loved me and missed me. That she felt that it was an appropriate time for her soul to go. Thea knew so many intimate details about our life that were so incredibly specific. Then the most wonderful thing happened!! Opal shared that she wanted to come back to me. That she knew I would need her for the next chapter of my life. I couldn't believe it. Another

lifetime with my soul mate. At that moment I felt like I took my grief off my body like a heavy blanket. Thea knew down to the DAY that Opal would be reborn. My new dog Nora is two years old now, and she and Opal are so alike that I have to explain to people that she's a different dog!

Signs From Spirit

Animals who have passed away know how important it is for their humans to know that they are still around, so they will often send their humans signs of that fact in their day-to-day life. Signs from spirits can really be anything, but the following are quite common:

✦ Subtle physical sensations of their presence. Chills, a sensation of warmth, a sensation of the animal lying next to you. A sensation of the animal bumping into you.

✦ Sounds from the animal's presence, such as the sound of the animal walking in the home.

✦ Visuals of the animal, such as their human seeing them out of the corner of their eye, seeing orbs of light in the room, or seeing their animal pop up visually in their mind unexpectedly.

✦ Finding seemingly random coins in significant spots.

✦ Finding feathers in significant spots.

✦ The animal's name popping up serendipitously; for example, the human randomly meeting another animal with the same name.

✦ Creatures—like butterflies, dragonflies, hummingbirds— showing up at significant times or coming closer than usual.

✦ Other unusual wildlife coming closer than usual.

✦ Having dreams in which the animal shows up.

✦ Electronics or electricity acting odd and going haywire at significant moments.

✦ Other pets seeing them around and reacting to them.

✦ Other events of synchronicity.

With signs, the animal's soul is working behind the scenes on the other side to align events in a way so that you happen to come across their signs at the right moment. With signs such as wildlife coming closer than usual, some people wonder if it's the animal's soul that has reincarnated into the bird or butterfly that they keep seeing, but that's not it. What is actually happening is that the animal's soul is influencing that wildlife to come closer to you, to try to catch your attention and make you think of them. Signs from your animal companions could be very much out of the ordinary, and are not always something related to the list above.

In my own personal experience, my passed beloved animals love to send signs involving their names. For example, a few years ago, I was teaching a class on animal communication in person at some local stables. During the class I had my students connect to a passed horse, named Petra, who was very special to me. When I got home from the class later that evening, I checked my phone and there was a notification from one of my apps that said, "Petra welcomes you to Portland Afterlife Meetup." This was a group I had requested to join a week or so before. What are the odds that someone named Petra (not a common name here) would send me a welcome to a group about the afterlife, right after I had my students connect to a special horse named Petra who is in the afterlife? It was a beautiful little hello from her.

One thing that can be difficult for us, when it comes to signs, is that we will start to overthink everything that could be a potential sign, and then, as a result, we take none of those signs to heart. If this tends to happen to you, you might find it helpful to decide yourself on a specific sign that you would love your animal companion to send you. It might be something random, like blue butterflies, or something as specific and obscure as a reference to Dolly Parton because your cat's name was Jolene after the song. Once you decide on a specific sign, you can ask your passed animal companion to send you the sign within the next few days, to show you that they really are around you. They will do their very best to send you that sign in some shape or form.

The topic of signs is important for us because it is a way in which we can continue our connection with our own animal companions, even outside of a mediumship session, and it's a way for the animal to show us that we are truly never alone.

Favorite Memories

An animal might bring up their favorite memories with their human, in part to show gratitude for those things, but also because it helps give the person something to focus on that is uplifting, healing, and positive, rather than the traumatic, guilt-ridden moments their humans may have been focusing on in the aftermath of a beloved animal's passing. A person who is grieving will naturally be overly focused on the ways in which they feel they failed their animal, or the ways in which the situation was not ideal. However, the animal who passed will often show us in readings that there was so much joy in their life that far outweighed the parts that weren't ideal. They often want their humans to focus on the fun and uplifting parts of their life and remember them in those ways. This can also be a very healing aspect of a reading.

Other important topics the animal might bring up: Their greater role in their human's life. The lessons they were trying to help their humans learn, or the challenges they supported their humans through. The animal might also want to talk about their human's current living pets, and perhaps give guidance about any situations involving them. Maybe they want to give their blessing for their human to bring another animal into their life. Maybe they will be part of that process, in which case they might have some ideas for what kind of animal it should be, and what characteristics the animal will have.

The following is an experience a client had connecting to her dog Shazi after she had passed away:

> Three days after my beloved dog Shazi died, I happened to
> have an appointment booked with Thea. I had scheduled
> the session over a month prior, before I knew Shazi was sick,

in hopes of getting more information about her worsening nighttime anxiety. I had taken her to the vet, who didn't see any glaring physical issues, so, on a whim, I found Thea on the internet and decided I'd see if she could help.

On the day of the appointment, I texted Thea to let her know that Shazi had passed away just a few days earlier. She gave me the option to cancel without charge or to go ahead with the appointment and try to connect with Shazi on the other side. I felt a tug on my insides, urging me to move forward with the session, so I did.

Having never received the services of a medium or animal psychic before, I had my doubts. I was heartbroken and missing Shazi with my whole being. The thought of connecting with her again, even for one hour, was incredibly compelling. It was like I'd been dying of thirst and had just been offered a glass of water. But another part of me was suspicious. Even though I was spiritual and open to the idea of mediumship, the stakes felt high. I was terrified of believing things that weren't true, simply because I was so desperate for them to be real. I knew I was vulnerable in my grief, and, as a result, I had my guard up, staying alert for red flags or confirmation bias.

As soon as I invited Thea into my home, I immediately became more relaxed. After explaining the process, she began connecting. There wasn't much fanfare or buildup; she closed her eyes and after a moment said, "Oh, is she a bit bossy?" I laughed and thought to myself, Yep, that's her. You dialed the right number. Shazi had, and apparently still has, a very distinct, strong personality. She was stubborn and regal; she demanded a certain level of respect. She was, in a word, bossy. As Thea continued to describe her, this immovable personality that I'd been missing so much came into the room, and I could feel Shazi as if she were sitting on the couch right next to me. In spite of myself, I let my doubts melt away, and I took the glass of water I'd been offered.

Thea relayed various specific events and circumstances Shazi and I had been through together. She named health issues Shazi had during her life and cross-country moves we'd made together. Shazi wanted me to know that I could rearrange the house however I wanted (I had organized the layout with her mobility issues in mind). She told me she felt well taken care of, even in the times I'd been unsure if I was making the right choices for her.

At one point, Thea asked, "Is there something about you not wanting to go upstairs?" I told her that, in the days since Shazi's passing, I had, in fact, been hesitant to go upstairs. By the time we moved into the house, Shazi could no longer make it upstairs, so she had never been in my bedroom. I had even been sleeping on the couch for the past few months so that she wouldn't have to be downstairs alone. After she died, I had the weird fear that, if Shazi's spirit was still around, she might be stuck on the first floor. Not knowing anything about the physics or rules on the other side, I was afraid that her spirit would not be able to follow me up there. It was such a relief when Thea responded that Shazi could connect with me anytime, anywhere, and she would be sticking around for quite a while. My uncertainty around death had led me to overanalyze all kinds of strange details like this, and now I could finally feel some of this anxiety letting up.

In regard to her death, Shazi brought forward some things she wanted to acknowledge—that she had declined very quickly, that it had been the right time for her to go, and that her transition to the other side had been smooth. I asked Thea if there was anyone who helped her across. After a moment, she said Shazi was showing her that several people were there to help her, many of whom Shazi hadn't met. My eyes welled up with more tears. In the moments before Shazi died, I had said a prayer asking my relatives and loved ones who'd passed to help her across. I knew that most of them hadn't known her, but I didn't want Shazi to be alone. It made my heart feel so full to know that they had heard me and had come to help her.

Shazi was not necessarily the most cuddly, overly affectionate dog, but our bond had felt incredibly strong. Through Thea, she communicated that, as stubborn as she had been sometimes, she loved me profoundly and always had. Of course, I knew that she loved me, but to hear it out loud with such specificity and certainty was something I never thought I'd get. And it brought me immeasurable peace to know that she was fully aware of how much love and gratitude I had for her, too.

After that session, everything changed. I had gotten answers to fundamental questions that I thought were unanswerable. For decades, I'd been terrified that the people and animals I'd loved and lost were just . . . gone. It made me scared of dying and scared of living; this fear was my shadow for years.

After that session, those feelings of fear and emptiness vanished. The way I understood the world and my place in it shifted fundamentally. The dark heaviness I'd felt in my core had dissipated and given way to spaciousness and light. My grieving process was totally transformed. Instead of battling dread and anxiety, worrying where Shazi was or if she was okay, I now had the space to mourn her and honor her. I was still completely devastated by her passing, and it took a while to learn how to be okay without her physical presence. Even a year later, I still miss her every single day. But it doesn't feel like I've lost her anymore; it feels like I am getting to know her in a new way. At one point, Thea had said, "She wants you to know, she's much more than just a dog." I can feel her around me often, supporting me and occasionally lending me some of her stubbornness and fortitude when I need a little strength. And I can sense that she is so much more than just a dog. But I knew that before she died, too.

Allowing the Animal's Soul to Guide the Session

In previous chapters we've talked about how, if you are doing a reading for someone else and connecting to living animals, it is often helpful to allow time for the animal's human to ask their own questions. With living animals, I recommend following a 50/50 model: Half of the session should be spent inviting the animal to take the lead, and then with the remaining time you can open it up to their human's questions. There is often some troubleshooting needed in a session with a living animal that requires the human to participate a little and ask questions or clarify. When connecting to animals who have passed, however, there isn't the same need for troubleshooting behavioral issues.

When you are doing a reading for someone else and connecting to their passed animals, the session is going to be much more impactful if you leave less time for questions and allow the animal's soul to take the lead for most of the time. I might leave ten to fifteen minutes at the end of the session for any questions the human might have. The animal is going to already know what their humans are wondering about, or what specific guilt they are holding on to, or what questions they might have. They might not always address all the questions their human has, but most of the time they will in some form, if given enough time in the session to do so. If we can allow the animal's soul time to bring those things up themselves, it also shows the human that their animal is still connected to them, and can feel their thoughts and know what's in their heart, despite not having a physical body anymore.

Connecting to Your Own Passed Animals

The wonderful thing about souls on the other side is that they can feel anytime you think of them, and they can hear anytime you talk to them. Just as living animals don't understand the literal words you are saying, but do understand the energy behind your words (what you intend to communicate), the same goes for those who have passed away. That means you do not need a dedicated medium to tell your passed animals anything. If you wish to get something off your chest, or just tell them how much you love and miss them, you can tell them out loud or in your mind, and they will hear you.

Most people, however, also want to feel their connection to their own passed animals and have a two-way conversation with them. When connecting to them yourself, it is very important to remember that your own grief and feelings of guilt can easily color, cloud, or twist the information coming through. A true connection with your beloved passed animals will always feel uplifting and loving, never angry or accusing toward you. Those on the other side have a much broader perspective of the situation of their passing, and are incredibly understanding of the decisions made and the surrounding circumstances. If what you are feeling in their communication is depressing, scary, hurtful, or accusing, then it's likely that your own thoughts and feelings are getting in the way of the connection. If that is the case, it might be best to wait to connect with your animal companion until you have more fully processed your grief.

Many want to know how soon after the animal's passing are they going to be available to connect. While an animal that has passed might appreciate a little bit of time to settle into the spirit-world, most are able to connect to their humans again just fine soon after passing, some even the same day as passing. However, you still might not be able to feel them around that early, even if the animal is around you and trying to let you know they're OK. It's less about giving the spirit time to settle in, and more about giving yourself a chance to process the initial intense grief that happens. If you don't give yourself a chance to process that initial grief, it's as if that grief becomes a fog lingering around you, making it harder to notice your animal companion there. The same can be a factor if you try to connect to your passed animal through a medium. The initial grieving stage can make it hard to be present and open enough for a successful session with a medium. However, it can vary from person to person. Sometimes a person will have strong connections to their own animals the day after their passing, perhaps because the soul was ready and the living person happened to be in the right state of mind. Overall, I recommend that you give yourself a bit of time, perhaps a few weeks or a couple of months even, before trying to connect to your own passed animals. And be patient with yourself if you don't have a successful first try. It doesn't mean that the animal isn't there ready to connect. You might just need to give yourself a bit more time first to clear some of the fog of the grief.

When connecting, such as in the exercise below, it's important to keep an open mind to what might come through, and not overthink it too much. Relax your logical thinking brain and allow your beloved animal to connect to you however they wish to do so. Even if what comes through feels like you might just be making it up, go with it. You can engage your logical brain again after the exercise, but for now you have to suspend your disbelief in order to allow for a genuine connection.

In this exercise we are not necessarily placing our awareness above us, but rather inviting the animal soul into our energy field. This way you can get a clearer sense of what it feels like when that particular soul is connecting to you. Each soul feels a little different when they connect. You can think of this as each soul's energy has its own energy-signature. Getting to know each soul's unique energy is helpful, so that if they connect to you at a later time while you are doing your day-to-day tasks, you can recognize their energy more easily.

Before doing the exercise, it can be a good idea to write down some questions you want the animal to answer for you. Here are some suggestions for good topics to ask them about. You can write down the questions beforehand, and you can tell the animal out loud that you'd love to hear the answers to these if possible. Remember: Even if they passed away and don't have a physical body anymore, they can hear you just fine.

✦ What are some of their favorite memories from their life?

✦ What they are up to on the other side?

✦ Who they are with? Have they met others?

✦ What signs do they try to send you?

✦ Do they have any messages for you?

You want to make sure that you keep your questions lighthearted, like those above. I don't recommend asking questions such as "Did this thing that I did—or didn't do—in some way contribute to your passing?" It's so easy for our own grief to creep in, making it hard to stay objective with questions like that. If you are still in detective mode about what happened in terms of their passing, and trying to figure out why things happened the way they did, I recommend that you schedule a session with a separate animal communicator. Your own brain is likely to kick in during high-pressure questions like that, and it will be hard to separate out what is from the animal and what is from your own mind.

The following is the experience from a husband and wife, who came to me for a phone session hoping to connect to their recently deceased cat. They were surprised to hear that they had many more animals showing up for them, including animals who had passed many years ago. A while after their session, they also got to experience their cat connect to them directly without any help from a medium.

Our first consultation with Thea occurred right after the death of our cat Tye. We were very distraught over his passing and were looking for some level of comfort and reassurance. We had worked with another communicator in the past, but had become concerned about that person's lack of accuracy in more recent years. We didn't tell Thea that we had other animals who had passed previously. We only told her that we had a cat who had recently passed and that his name was Tye. When she started talking to Tye, she said that there were so many others showing up that it was "like a circus." She was having a hard time telling everyone apart! We had no idea that others would potentially show up during this consultation. Everyone showed up! Even a beloved lovebird whom I had for only two years over twenty years prior to the conversation. It was like a family reunion that we didn't know was possible. Thea did connect with Tye, but very shortly after, Thea said that there was a dog who was coming through, one who had been very connected to me in her life. She was extraordinarily specific about this dog's personality (including that she was "dancing around happily," which is exactly what she often did when she met new people), and described aspects of her life that were 100 percent accurate. We knew that it was the dog I considered to be my "soul mate," whose passing had traumatized me desperately many years prior, named Chloe. Chloe told Thea, "Tye is fine, I'll take care of him, but I have some things to say." Chloe conveyed to Thea information that was deeply, deeply personal. She told her the unfortunate incidents that led to her passing, and the profound effect they had on me. She told her specifics about how she died, and the things we did to try to help her right until the end. It was unmistakable that the entity Thea was talking to was Chloe. Chloe then told Thea about the intense guilt that I had felt since her passing, and how even to that day, years later, I still carried it with me every day. It was hindering my ability to find happiness and contentment in my life in ways I did not even realize. She told me the things I didn't know I needed to hear to move past her death and my guilt and grief. Before Chloe handed the conversation back to Tye, she let me know that all the times I thought I "felt" her around me, I was right, because she is nearly always with me. To this day, I feel her with me all the time—dancing around me when I am happy, comforting me when I am sad or struggling, and enjoying the breeze when I drive with the windows down (as she did when she was alive). This knowledge brought me peace that I didn't know I was missing in my life.

When Thea came back to Tye, he stated his appreciation for our care (he was only with us for a short time, but we treated him as though we had him since kittenhood). During the conversation, Tye kept focusing on a lizard. Thea stated several times, "Are you sure neither of you has a lizard you are or were connected to?" But neither of us had ever had a lizard or known anyone who did, so we let it go. The conversation ended shortly after, and my husband and I sat in silence staring at each other for a while afterward, in complete shock over what we had just experienced. Fast-forward to a year later. We were in Tahiti and decided on the spur of the moment to get our first tattoos in traditional Polynesian symbolism. I got an eagle ray, and my husband got a gecko. A few weeks later, when we got back, we were talking about the tattoo experience, and we both heard, "HEY, LIZARD!!!" in our heads at the same time. We both looked at each other open-mouthed . . .Tye had connected with us on his own, about the lizard he had insisted on during his session.

This session with Thea fundamentally changed how we see the universe. When our cattle dog Emmy passed away a few short years later, it was so very sad, but at the same time we knew that Thea would be able to connect with her, so it wasn't the last time we would talk to her. We also knew that "goodbye for now" doesn't mean "goodbye forever," and that she would still be around us, keeping us company and guiding us. We no longer see death as the end, but rather the beginning of a different phase, one where we can still keep in touch in some way. This knowledge gives us peace and comfort, especially in times of stress. We understand our place in the universe, and we know that we have others there, helping us and cheering for us.

Exercise:
Connecting to Your Own Passed Animals

Take a few deep breaths, feel yourself centered and grounded, and now bring your awareness to the center of your chest, to your heart center, feeling the light there big and bright. And now expand that light at the center of your chest, either through visualizing it or just setting the intention and knowing that the energy will follow. Let that light expand out a couple of feet beyond your body, so that it surrounds you. This is your energy field. Take a moment to just feel what that feels like, with only your own energy there. Now you are going to mentally call on your beloved animal and ask them to step into your energy field so you can sense what their soul feels like now.

Notice how your energy field feels different now, or where your attention is drawn to in your energy field around you. Maybe it feels warmer to you in a certain spot. Maybe you receive some visual impressions in your mind's eye, or words in your head, or just emotions coming through from the animal. Maybe you just get a knowing that they are there. Maybe you suddenly feel drawn to one side of your body.

Then ask your animal to step out of your energy field briefly and notice what it feels like now when it is just your energy. Don't worry, they're not going anywhere. Allow yourself a moment to feel only your own energy, and then ask your animal to step back into your energy field again. Notice how it changes, what it feels like, or any impressions that you're getting. Remember that their presence will likely come across as subtle. You are getting used to what their energy feels like now that they don't have a physical body anymore. You can ask them to step in and out of your energy field however many times you need, in order to discern the subtle difference when they are present.

If you are a very visual person, you can also try visualizing being in a room or garden, and inviting your animal to spend time with you there. Notice how do they interact with you there? Once you have gotten a sense of what their energy feels like now, you can take a moment to fully greet your animal companion. You can now tell them anything and everything you want to share with them. You might ask them your questions. Or just spend a moment in each other's presence, enjoying their company again.

Once you are ready, you can thank your animal companion for connecting, you can ask them to continue to visit you whenever they want, and you can let them know you will be on the lookout for their presence.

Grief

We tend to grow very close to our animal companions while they are with us. For many of us, they become part of the family, and for some of us, they are the only family we have. They are often the ones we spend the most time with in our life. Whenever we are home, they are home with us, sometimes glued to our side. They become emotional support, they fulfill important roles in our life, and I would say that most love us unconditionally.

An animal companion passing is often similar to the experience of losing a child. Of course, it's not the same, but there are certain aspects of both that are very similar. This is because we are responsible for our animals, for feeding them, for training them, for taking care of their health, for making sure they are happy and comfortable. Because they are unable to talk to us as humans do, we are often in a position of having to make big choices for them, usually just based on guesses about what the animal is experiencing and what they want. We might have issues of finances and other surrounding circumstances that make it difficult to make the decisions we would like to. Yet, due to our responsibility for our animals, their passing often feels like a personal failure on our part to keep them alive and to keep them happy and comfortable, even if logically we know that it isn't fully in our hands.

Add to that the unconditional love that animals tend to radiate toward us. And we know that being human, we don't always show that unconditional love back. Right now you might be feeling guilt for not always acting in a way that radiated your unconditional love for your animals. But, despite logically knowing that we are human, and therefore fallible, we hold ourselves to unrealistic standards when it comes to taking care of our beloved animals. So, the grief of losing an animal can go extremely deep, sometimes deeper than losing a human family member.

Feelings of guilt come up often for people in their grieving process. Feelings of failing our animal companions. Uncertainty. Worries about whether or not we made the right decisions for them. Feeling like we should have done more to help them, even if we know logically there wasn't anything else we could do. Regret about not doing more of the things we know the animal loved. The hole in our life from losing their physical presence around us is difficult to get used to, and it becomes a reminder of all of those feelings of guilt, regret, and loss.

The grief that people go through when an animal companion passes away is very real, and unique in such a way that we often feel a bit silly about how much we grieve. We don't necessarily talk about loss, grief, or death much in our culture, and especially not when it comes to losing animals. So people often feel very lost and lonely when they go through that, and connecting to their beloved animals again can be a wonderfully healing experience. A reading with an animal medium or connecting to your passed animals on your own can allow space for that grief, and space for healing.

Animals who have passed *want* to come through and connect with their humans again because they still love and care about them. They want to let their humans know that they are okay. They might see their humans holding on to feelings of guilt or deep regret about things that the animal doesn't want them to feel guilty or regret about. The animal might want to share their own perspective on what happened, to help alleviate that guilt or regret.

Living animals tend to view death as something very normal: Many of them are hunters by nature, and, in general, animals are often aware of the other side already. Many animals can feel or see people and animals who have already passed, hanging around their humans. Often when an animal gets closer to their time of passing (when they are deathly ill or dying), they will become aware of those on the other side who are getting ready to greet them when they cross over. This might be people or animals they knew in life, or people and animals who are connected to their human and who they didn't know in life.

Since animals are so comfortable with the idea of death, they don't tend to be afraid of it. They have a sense of what it will be like when they cross over, and they know that they aren't going to disappear forever. They might, however, be worried about their humans, because they feel their humans going through so much emotional turmoil about it even before they pass, or they know their human is worried, and so they worry about them. People who have terminally ill or dying animals often start their grieving process well before the animal has passed. The animal can feel their human's grief already. The intense emotions the human is going through can sometimes be unsettling to the animal, which makes them exhibit fearful or worried behavior, but it's usually only connected to their worry about their human, not about actually dying.

Just because a living animal is comfortable with the idea of death does not mean that they don't grieve when their own humans or when their animal friends pass. Just as with us, even if we know that the soul continues after the body dies, we still grieve the loss of our own loved ones. It's a big transition that often calls for healing and compassion, even for animals.

An animal who has passed gets a full overview of the circumstances surrounding their passing. They know what their human's intentions were. They know intimately how much they are loved. They know and understand much more than we do about the hows and whys of what happened. They also know that they were going to pass one way or another, and they will often want to point out the positives of how they passed.

Because they continue to love and care for their humans, even as they are in the spirit world, they want to bring healing and understanding to those humans, and also want to prove to them that they are still around. That even though they are not there physically anymore, they still are involved and interested in their life, and continue to support them in whatever way they can. They might want to prove that their humans are never truly alone.

They also want to show their gratitude for the things that were done for them, in life and also after their passing. We get caught up in all the ways we feel we failed them, when what our animal companions want to focus on is all the ways in which we were there for them and the ways they've been honored.

A few years ago, I would do readings at local metaphysical fairs a couple times a year. One time a woman came to my booth, wanting to connect to a childhood dog who had passed away. Her dog not only came through, but ended up also giving some guidance on how the woman could honor her memory and ultimately feel closer to her:

> I will never forget my first session with Thea at a local metaphysical fair. I had never had a reading with an animal communicator before, so I wasn't sure what to expect. What I received was more than I thought possible. She connected to my sweetest pup who grew up with me and comforted me through my darkest times while I dealt with my genetic disorder and its symptoms. Due to my health, I was unable to be with my pup when she passed. I had agonized and felt guilty for not being there for years! Thea helped me find out that my pup held no ill will toward me, only love.

A few days before my reading, I found out that there were necklaces you could buy that were little vials meant for pets' ashes. They had little paw prints on them, too. I almost bought one of the necklaces but didn't. At the end of the session, Thea asked if I had one last question. I asked her if there was one thing that my pup would want me to do to honor her. Thea responded, wear her ashes. I started to cry, I couldn't believe that the necklace I was thinking about purchasing was exactly what my pup wanted me to do. It helped me realize the love and companionship I still had with my pup even though she was on the other side. I bought the necklace the next day, and whenever I wear it I feel closer to my pup than I could have ever hoped.

Compassion, Euthanasia, Timing

Euthanasia is one of those topics that can get complicated for humans, and it represents a decision that is extremely difficult to make. There are unfortunately ideas floating around in society about how euthanasia might interrupt the animal's karmic path, and somehow cause them to get stuck in between worlds. In every session I have done with animals who crossed by euthanasia, the animals see euthanasia as help in crossing over. Not as murder. They are never stuck between worlds. They cross over peacefully and quickly, and most animals I have connected to show gratitude for the help they got in crossing over, as they are aware that this was a difficult decision for their humans to make. Some have even pointed out the similarities with how some humans who are terminally ill choose to get assistance in dying (here in Oregon it's called "death with dignity").

On the flip side, not everybody chooses to use euthanasia, and not everybody gets a chance to even make that decision before their animal crosses over by other means. Euthanasia is an incredibly difficult decision, and not always the right one for everyone. Some animals do prefer to pass on their body's own time, without that being any more traumatic or horrible than euthanasia. Many animals pass unexpectedly. Again, these are things that are going to be very individual for each animal soul, and each situation, but since they have a complete overview of the choices and factors surrounding their passing, they are always incredibly understanding of the choices that were made for them, and they see the love behind the choices, as well as the bigger picture.

There also seems to be a certain divine timing in connection to an animal's passing. This is another big point of worry among humans, especially when there was euthanasia involved. Was it the right time? We see euthanasia as us making one big decision and taking that power away from the Divine, putting it in our own hands. What we often don't see is that our decisions are part of the bigger picture that we have no control over. The animal likely would have crossed over one way or another, whether or not it happened in that specific way. In many cases there is not much the human could have done to stop the animal from passing, because it was their soul's time to leave their body. Euthanasia can often make it a more peaceful passing.

We also tend to see the "right time" of passing as one specific second, and anything outside of that second is the "wrong time," when in reality souls often communicate that the right timing for their passing is a window that is sometimes even months long, so that any time within that window was appropriate for their passing.

When it comes to an animal's last days on earth, it's hard to ever feel that we made the "right" decision or took all the "right" steps. But what's most important to know is that when your animal passes, they know all about the love behind your decisions and your efforts to do right by them.

Some animals keep a chipper demeaner despite having serious life-threatening illnesses. These are the hardest ones to make a decision about euthanasia for, as they will still try to chug along even if their disease has progressed to a point where the animal is not able to move anymore. The following is the experience of a client, who helped her cat pass by euthanasia, and ended up doubting the decision she made as the guilt of her grief set in:

> Thea connected with our very sorely missed cat Sunshine.
> We had him euthanized as he was quickly deteriorating from
> cancer at age sixteen. I was feeling incredibly guilty and
> regretful as his mood and energy level were unaffected by his
> illness. I felt that we had let him down. I didn't tell Thea any
> of that, so when she said he communicated that he knew we
> made a mercy decision, I was so deeply healed. He assured
> me there was no hope of improving, and that he's grateful that
> we cared about his quality of life. We will always miss Sunshine
> tremendously, but knowing that he's not mad at us gave
> my husband and me some peace of mind. There have been
> incidents of Sunshine letting me know he's around. I strongly
> advise pet parents missing their babies to pay attention—
> they're letting you know they're nearby!

I believe the job of an animal medium is to simply be a translator for what the spirit of the animal wishes to communicate. It is not the medium's job to judge what happened, or insert their own opinion about what the person should have done, or what they should do. They are simply the medium through which information is given. Mediumship is about love, reunion, and healing. Because of the grief and serious topics brought up in sessions like this, in addition to being the medium through which the animal communicates, they are also the ones holding compassionate space for the healing to happen. In order to do this work, you need to be able to put your own personal opinions and beliefs to the side, in order to allow the spirit to show you what is true for them and what is important for them to talk about.

We always need to make sure that we push for the most accurate and clear information and do our best to do the animal justice as they come through. This is so the client can feel that their animal truly came through, so that they take the messages fully to heart. That's why we focus on doing evidential readings, so that the messages the animal has hold more weight for the human. That being said, you could do the most astounding reading ever with loads of amazingly accurate evidence and messages, and the person might still want more reassurance and evidence. Connecting to an animal can help, but it doesn't replace the grieving process. The animals might still be around us in spirit form, but there has still been a major change, and they will never be the same as they were before. Grief is the process of coming to terms with the fact that we don't have them here in the way we used to before they passed.

The grieving process is different for everyone. There's really no right or wrong to your feelings. They just are. I think it's important to know that you are not holding your pet's soul back by grieving. This is a common misconception I see—that when we continue to grieve an animal's passing, we are in some way holding the animal's soul back from their evolution or journey on the other side. That is absolutely not the case.

However, heavy and complicated grief can make it harder to feel our animal companions' presence around us. Grief can cloud a person's thinking and connection to the spirit world in general, at least in the initial period after an animal's passing. If you are feeling stuck in heavy grief and find it difficult to feel your animal companion's presence, it may be helpful to try to think of some fun memories you have with them, and the things you loved about them and things they did that lifted your spirits when they were alive. Taking some breaks from thinking about the heavy stuff, with some concentrated effort to think about the fun, lighthearted stuff, can be a powerful way to lift the fog of grief around you for a little bit, making it easier to feel your passed animals around you.

Ultimately, animal mediumship isn't always enough for everyone, and if you would like some extra support, therapy is absolutely a valid resource for pet loss. There are also pet loss support groups, as well as hotlines. Look in the back of this book for resources on pet loss and grief support groups.

✦

CHAPTER 7

Confidence

When you begin to become aware of subtle energy and open up to communication with animals living and passed, you might find that you start to become aware of other subtle energies around you. It can feel overwhelming to some people to perceive more and more through their psychic senses. If you want to develop your abilities—both as an animal communicator or elsewhere within the realm of psychic readings—it's important to have clear boundaries, so that you don't feel quite so overwhelmed by everything around you.

As I've previously mentioned, if you are in the right state of mind to perceive subtle energy, then what your awareness is on is what you're tuning in to. If you start to feel overwhelmed by your intuitive abilities, it can be a very useful practice to regularly bring your awareness back to yourself and back to your own body, so that you are not just tuning in to everything and anything around you all the time. You can bring your awareness back to yourself through meditation, or even just through a simple practice of calling back all your own energy from wherever in the world it just was and sending all foreign energy back to wherever it came from.

When it comes to mediumship and opening up to connect with passed beloved animals, some people start to feel overwhelmed by other spirits (passed humans and other passed animals) wanting to connect with them. This doesn't typically happen, but it can. If you start to feel overwhelmed by the spirit world, the good news is that you absolutely can learn to control it and learn to "turn it off" in a sense. Now, it doesn't function like a light switch; that is, you can't just turn on and turn off your abilities, per se. However, it has very much to do with where you place your awareness and also how clear your personal boundaries are.

If you consistently place your awareness on the spirit world a lot of the time, you are opening up to that realm, so naturally that's what you are connecting to. Let's say you find yourself wondering what passed loved ones are hanging around your friend, you are opening up to them, and you might find yourself connecting to them. Turning it "off" is simply about consciously focusing on the living world around you, bringing your awareness to your body, to the room around you, focusing on the chores you have to do, etc.

Boundaries

Having strong boundaries in place is very effective in controlling who gets to connect to you when, especially in terms of those on the other side. The good news is this: Just because you can connect to the spirit world does not mean that you have to. The thing is, though, that if you don't have a healthy sense of boundaries in your day-to-day life—if you can't say no to those in the living world—then you likely won't have healthy boundaries with those on the other side.

I believe strong boundaries come from a strong belief in your own worth. Because you are part of the Divine, you are already beyond worthy. You are worthy of not having to be overwhelmed by everything and everyone all the time. In the same way that you are worthy of having your own home and space to yourself, without strangers walking in the door at all hours of the day demanding your attention, you are worthy of having your space and energy to yourself without strangers in the spirit world demanding your attention at all hours of the day.

Developing Clarity

Hopefully, your interest in animal communication has been piqued, and maybe you want to expand your practice and dip your toes into connecting with other people's animals, too. Maybe you've reached out to friends with animals and asked to practice with them, or maybe you've joined a practice group online. Now what? Well, now you want to work on developing clarity in your communications!

Navigating the No

Let's say you are doing a reading for someone else, connecting to their animal, and their human says no—that the piece of information you just brought through about their animal doesn't make sense or that it's just plain wrong. Your stomach drops, you start sweating, and you immediately start questioning your own abilities. It can be jarring and scary to get a no to the information coming through. But I want you to know that it's very normal to get a no in a reading—it happens to everyone! Don't fear the no, and don't freak out! Use the no as an opportunity to clarify with the animal.

Text continues on page 188

Exercise:
Making a Boundaries List

I always recommend that people make a boundaries list. This is where you get clear on who you are okay connecting to, as well as when and where. You can also ask your spirit guides to help enforce your list. Getting clear on what's okay with you—and what's not okay with you—helps you shift your energy and helps you become more intentional about who you open up to on the other side. When you also believe that you are worthy of being able to decide that for yourself, that strengthens those boundaries further.

Here is an example of my own boundaries list:

In my own house, these types of spirits can connect with me:

✦ My own spirit guides

✦ My own loved ones (including passed animals)

✦ Angels; benevolent beings

✦ Spirit guides and loved ones of any clients I am connecting for, only during a session with said client

When I am out and about, these spirits can connect with me:

✦ Same as in my house, but may include spirit guides and loved ones of other people

When can these spirits connect with me?:

✦ Never when I am about to go to bed or while I am sleeping, unless it is a visit from my own loved ones or spirit guides in my dreams

Your own boundaries list might look different, and you might want to include other things on the list that are important to you. For example, you might also want to connect only to your own loved ones, and that is absolutely fine and you are absolutely allowed to decide that, and the spirit world must respect those boundaries. But, remember, you also have to believe that you are worthy of having your boundaries respected. If not, then boundaries have a tendency to become very fluid as a result. If you know that you are worthy of respect (because everybody is) and get to be in charge of yourself, then you get to decide when visiting hours are and who gets access to your energy and abilities.

If you get a no amid mostly yes answers, this might be what's going on:

✦ You might have misunderstood the animal and misinterpreted the information.

✦ Their human may have misunderstood the information, or just not realized in the moment what the info is referring to.

✦ Their human may have forgotten about the thing the animal is referencing (this happens a lot).

✦ The animal might be referencing something that their human doesn't know about.

✦ A different animal may be interrupting your reading, and you just don't notice it. This can happen when there are several animals in the same household together with the one you intended to communicate with. Remember: This can happen with an animal who has passed away, even if you intended to connect to a living animal, and vice versa.

First and foremost, any time you get a no, you will want to dive deeper into your connection with the animal, not clam up and retreat from the connection. Most of us are wired to shut down immediately when we get a no. You might still have a hard time trusting your own abilities and trusting that animal communication is even possible. When you get that no, the brain takes it as confirmation of your deepest fears!

But truly, the no does not mean failure. It just means that there has been some kind of miscommunication somewhere. It's a natural part of a reading, because it's all about communication, and communication is an imperfect process, even between two humans. Then add in an animal, and everyone has different styles of communication. It's not always going to flow without a hitch.

You Have to Be Willing to Be Wrong in Order to Be Right

Are you going to be wrong sometimes? Undoubtedly. Will you sometimes misinterpret the info coming through? Probably. And, also, that's okay! You are human and fallible. Nobody expects you to be perfect all the time (or at least I don't expect you to be). A reading doesn't need to be perfect in order for it to have amazing results for the animal and their human. A reading doesn't need to be perfect for it to have an amazing impact. Give yourself and your readings permission to be, not perfect, but amazing, whatever kind of amazing they need to be. That might be a subtle kind of amazing, or a jaw-dropping kind of amazing.

So how do we handle the no?

✦ Ask the animal to clarify what they mean. They might give you more information about the topic, so you and their human know what they're talking about. They might give you the information again, but in a different way.

✦ Clarify with their human what you are getting. What are the most important parts of what's coming through? Did you add something to it that wasn't there originally? Were you not clear enough, and maybe that confused the human? Did you remember to include all the details? Sometimes the human thinks you're talking about one thing, when really you're talking about something else. Does it feel like you are on the same page? Back up a few steps, begin to explain again what is coming through, and make sure that you and their human are on the same page.

✦ If the animal insists that the info is correct, tell their human and ask them to take note of it for now. They might see that it makes sense later.

✦ Ask their human if the information makes sense for another animal. If so, see if the animal has anything else they need to get off their chest, then thank that animal, disconnect from them, and connect to the animal you intended to connect with in the first place.

Either way, a no is helpful in a reading to show you where you need to clarify, and how to proceed. To see where you might have misinterpreted something, or where you need to push yourself to give more details, or where you might need to make sure that you are on the same page as their human. But remember, even though the information doesn't make sense to you right now, it very well might make sense later on.

What if you are getting mostly no's?

✦ You might be having an off day. If you are tired or sick, this can affect your readings.

✦ It may have been a different animal from the very start.

So how do we handle a reading when it's all off the mark?

✦ In the case of several animals living in the same household, if it was a different animal from the start, the only way you would know usually is if the information doesn't make sense about the animal you intended to talk to, and you'll just get a lot of no's from their human. Ask the human if the information makes sense for another animal in the house. If so, see what else that animal wants to communicate, then thank that animal, disconnect from them, and connect to the animal you intended to connect with in the first place.

✦ Check in with yourself—see if nerves are getting in the way, causing you to misinterpret, or if something else is distracting you from the reading. Acknowledge whatever it is, put it to the side for now, and take a moment to get back into a relaxed, but heightened state. Expand your energy again, reconnect with the animal, and ask them to share with you something about themselves that helps identify who they are.

✦ If you are simply not able to connect to an animal, that's okay! Just acknowledge it and be honest with their human, and either reschedule or refer them to another animal communicator who might be a better fit. Most intuitives I know will, every once in a while, encounter someone or something that they have difficulty connecting with, and this happens in the animal communication field as well. Many choose not to charge for the reading if they aren't able to connect at all. Remember, though, that a few pieces misinformation is okay and normal, and should be expected in a reading. It's a whole different thing if the entire reading is off, and none of the information that comes through makes sense about any of their other animals, living or passed.

✦ Make sure to be well-rested and well-fed before doing readings! Make sure to meditate and ground yourself beforehand. If you are doing several readings in one day, be sure to schedule at least fifteen to thirty minutes between sessions to take a break and care for yourself (stretch, snack, clear your energy, get some tea). If you feel sick, it might be better to reschedule for when you are feeling better.

Sometimes, the human you are doing the reading for will be so set on connecting to just one particular animal that they might not remember or recognize others who might be trying to communicate. Many people who receive a reading will have a mental list of things they expect to hear about in a session, and anything that doesn't match that list they might automatically say no to, even if the information is technically correct. This includes animals they are not expecting to hear from. To help your readings flow as smoothly as possible, it's best to remind the person to keep their mind open to who might show up, and that animals they were not expecting to hear from might come through, too. That way, they are aware of the possibility, and they aren't as married to their own agenda, so that we can allow for the best reading experience possible.

Accuracy

Some people have a tendency to hold back the information coming through from the animal, because they're worried that it will be wrong. This was definitely my problem when I started doing readings for others. The fear of being inaccurate in readings often stems from the underlying concept that there is a right answer and a wrong answer. This concept is very loaded for many people, and can start a cascade of thoughts, such as "What if that was wrong?," "Am I doing this right?," "Am I good enough?," "What is the animal's human thinking about me right now?," etc. These are all very noisy thoughts that make it hard to listen to the animal. When developing your animal communication abilities (or any intuitive abilities), it is helpful to change this concept of right and wrong into simply *what is and what isn't*. It is a subtle, but important, distinction. In a reading, you are simply taking a peek at *what is*, meaning what you are seeing/sensing/feeling/knowing/hearing through your psychic senses as you connect to the animal. Part of the work is getting away from the notion of performing, as you want to bring your attention back to your connection with the animal and what you are experiencing.

The other important benefit of the what is/what isn't concept is that it shifts you into acceptance mode of what you are sensing, because you are bringing your focus back to the information as you are sensing it. Acceptance mode is the exact state you want to be in during a reading. It is also called "being in the flow." This is where whatever you are getting through your psychic senses just is, and you are not fighting the information coming through, editing it, or throwing it out. Whether or not the information is correct, you cannot deny that the information exists, as you experience it through your senses.

Let's say that during a reading you are connecting to a cat, and all of a sudden you see a goat in your mind's eye, next to the cat. Whether or not the cat's humans actually have a goat, it is still a fact that you are seeing the goat there in your mind's eye. There could be a whole range of reasons that you are seeing the cat with a goat. The point is to always bring your focus back to what you are sensing through your psychic senses, and make it a rule to always accept and acknowledge what is coming through, so you can stay in the flow. From there you can ask the cat to clarify why they are showing you the goat. If you start fighting the fact that you're seeing the goat, you get in your own way, the information starts slowing down, and it makes for a terrible connection with the cat.

As readers, so much of a reading is guided by what we believe is possible. We might have expectations, ideas of what the reading is going to be like, or how it would look if it's successful. But often those ideas get in the way of what would be truly transformational for the client. It makes us fight the flow of energy and information, and not let through everything that wants to come through. The more we try to control the reading, the more our efforts constrict the energy of the reading, and the more our brain tends to muddle things.

A good spiritual practice before doing readings is to remind yourself to soften your heart, soften your mind, and open up to anything and everything that needs to come through, even if it doesn't match your ideas of what a reading "should look like." Release your own ideas to allow for the best reading possible.

Intention

If you find that it's still difficult to get around this fear of inaccuracy, it might be helpful to check your intentions for doing readings. Being correct should never be the intention for doing a reading, because then you've made the reading about performing. The main problem with this is that it directs your focus to how the animal's human is reacting to the "performance." Remember earlier when we talked about expanding and directing our awareness to what we're reading? When doing an animal communication reading, your awareness should be on the animal you are connecting to. When you begin to think of the reading as a performance, your awareness shifts to the person you're reading for and how they are reacting, and you're not connecting to the animal as strongly.

A more useful intention for doing readings is to be of service to the animal, their human, and their relationship. Shifting your focus from performing to being of service directs your awareness to the energy you are connecting to, and ultimately to doing your job of connecting and being a translator, strengthening your connection to the animal.

It might be a good idea to make it a habit to state your intention of being of service before a reading, either mentally or out loud, to help you focus your awareness in the right direction. If you find yourself getting nervous before or during a reading, always bring it back to being of service.

Next Steps

If you want to continue exploring your own animal communication abilities, I highly recommend practicing as much as you can, both with your own animals and with friends' animals. Get practice with animals you don't know well, so you can get feedback from their humans on the information that came through. If you can take a class in animal communication, make sure you have opportunities to practice in the class, so you can make strides with your development. It really is through the practice that you develop and improve your abilities to be of service for animals everywhere. Each animal is so delightfully unique and wonderful, both in the life they live, the perspective they have, and the way they communicate. Each experience we get to have communicating with animals teaches us something new. You're going to do most of your learning not from a book, but from the animals themselves!

✦

Final Thoughts

My childhood cat Klara, the one my dad secretly got us when I was ten, died some years ago now. It was one of the most brutal losses for me, despite knowing that she's still connected to me in spirit, but she did send me a little sign from the other side. I had been thinking about her, missing her presence, and then just a few days later, one of my social media accounts was hacked, and whoever hacked my account changed my name to Olga, which was Klara's name before we adopted her. I had experienced enough by then to know there are no coincidences when it comes to signs from Spirit. My current cat companions, Humphrey and Gilly, love to support my work and will lie next to me any time I do readings from home. One of their jobs is as assistant professors in the classes I teach. Gilly is still an enthusiastic communicator, and will still hijack conversations even if my students are supposed to be talking to Humphrey.

One of my favorite parts about doing animal communication readings, beyond just the fun and potential snuggles, is that it demonstrates just how vast all beings are. Animals have intricate inner lives and unique roles in the world. There is so much more to them than what meets the eye, and probably more than we can even imagine. Animal communication and mediumship have also shown me how amazing humans are, and how this wonderful skill is available to everyone as the basis of who we all are: spirits in bodies, who are all connected to the natural world around us.

Glossary

Animal Communication: When someone connects to an animal (usually still living) and acts as a translator, bringing through information about the animal and its life without having known the information beforehand. We call this doing a "reading."

Mediumship Reading: When someone connects to a person or animal who has passed away, bringing through information about them, without having known the information beforehand. This is also called doing a "reading."

Reader: The person doing the "reading."

Spirit Guide: Loosely refers to a category of spiritual (nonphysical) beings who take an interest in our well-being and who wish to help us reach our full potential. Will often include animal spirits as well. This can sometimes include human loved ones and animal companions who have crossed over, but this is not always the case.

The Three Main Types of Intuitive Communication

All of these go under the umbrella of "animal communication."

The first involves connecting telepathically to the animal's current incarnation and personality. This usually focuses on how the animal is doing and what sorts of challenges they've been having lately. The benefit of this kind of connection is that it is a true conversation with the animal in which they are an equal participant. When the communicator asks a question, the animal can then respond to their human both in the conversation and with their behavior afterwards. This is often seen as a practical kind of connection, about the animal's day-to-day life with their human and how to improve that.

The second method of communication involves connecting to an animal's higher self. This type of reading tends to focus on information about the bigger lessons in life that the animal is here to teach their humans. This method can be helpful for deepening the relationship between the animal and their human, and it can also help the human work through and heal the issues they're dealing with in life.

The third method of communication happens when you connect on a psychic level to the animal's energy. This is not a telepathic connection (meaning, it's not a conversation), but more of an exploration of the animal's energy on your own initiative. This method can be helpful for identifying things that the animal isn't consciously aware of, for example getting a clearer sense of health issues in the animal's body.

The focus of this book is on the first method: active communication with the animal. However, there are situations where the other methods will be more effective.

Resources

Guided Meditations

www.theahealer.com/book-meditations

At this site, associated with this book, you can access several guided meditations that can help you develop your abilities as a communicator. This site also includes a basic grounding and connecting meditation, an expanding awareness meditation, an animal spirit guide meditation, and a meditation for connecting to your own passed animals.

Further Support for Challenging Animal Behaviors

Animal behaviorists and trainers that use gentle training methods are great resources to use in combination with communication and can provide useful tools to support your animal companions. The following books are helpful resources for working with challenging animal behaviors when animal communication isn't enough.

American College of Veterinary Behaviorists. *Decoding Your Dog: Explaining Common Dog Behaviors and How to Prevent or Change Unwanted Ones.* New York: Houghton Mifflin Harcourt Publishing Co., 2014.

Dunbar, Ian. *Before and After Getting Your Puppy: The Positive Approach to Raising a Happy, Healthy, and Well-Behaved Dog.* Novato: New World Library, 2004.

Johnson-Bennett, Pam. *Starting from Scratch: How to Correct Problem Behaviors in Your Adult Cat.* London: Penguin Books, Ltd, 2007.

Weston, Hannah, and Rachel Bedingfield. *Connection Training: The Heart and Science of Positive Horse Training.* Denver: Connection Training, Ltd., 2019.

Pet Loss Support

https://www.aplb.org/

This website is run by the Association of Pet Loss and Bereavement. They have many resources listed on their website, include a list of free pet loss support groups.

https://www.humananimalbondtrust.org/

This website has a helpful list of pet loss support hotlines, in addition to other resources.

Acknowledgments

Writing a book has been such an unexpected and wonderful experience that would not have been possible without all of my clients and students over the years, who have opened themselves up to me and my work, as well as shared their amazing animal companions with me. I have learned so much from each and every one of you. I want to further thank my clients who so generously offered to share their experiences of our sessions together so I could add them to the book. I wish I had space to include all of them, but please know that every single one of them is stored in my heart and will be cherished forever.

I would like to thank all the mediums, psychics, and animal communicators who have come before me, who have shared their gifts and paved the way for this type of work to be more accepted in the world. My own path was ignited when I met Lady Christopher Barrett and Frannie Hoffman. Thank you for inspiring 12-year-old me and introducing me to the amazing world of mediumship and animal communication. Thank you for showing me what's possible.

This book would likely not have happened if it weren't for the amazing astrologer Zy at 3rdEyeZy and the amazing medium Renee Madsen Terrill. Both gave me readings individually, and both stuck to their guns when they predicted I would be writing a book on animal communication, despite my great misgivings and less-than-enthusiastic response. Without their predictions, I probably would not have been open to the idea of writing this book when the opportunity presented itself. Renee is also an excellent mediumship teacher who I was lucky to learn from when I first started developing my abilities. I would also like to extend a big heartfelt thanks to medium Alyson Gannon. I would be nowhere if not for her practice circles, generosity, encouragement, and mentorship.

I'm extremely grateful to Leah D'Ambrosio and Kathleen Prasad for all of their support. Years ago, before I even started to develop as an animal communicator,

I read Kathleen's book on animal reiki. Even though animal reiki is quite different than animal communication, Kathleen's philosophy of letting the animal lead the session has been hugely influential to my animal communication. And Leah has been the biggest supporter and believer in what I do and teach, whose friendship I cherish deeply. I would also like to mention another dear friend, Priscila De Macedo, who is an amazing psychic in her own right. In addition to showing me what true friendship is like, Priscila gave me a sense of community when I desperately needed one within the spiritual field, and she inspired me to come out as a medium and animal communicator. Also I would like to send a big thanks to my friend Peter Fogtdal who gave me his expert author advice as I was considering taking on this book project.

I would like to recognize the invaluable assistance of Robin Skov. Thank you for helping lessen the load of admin overwhelm in the past few years, helping me put together my courses, offering your animal companions as assistant teachers, and generally being a light in the world.

I would like to extend my deepest gratitude to my editor Kate Zimmermann, who took a chance on me. Not only did she offer me this project, but her expert editing has been instrumental in cobbling it together to be a cohesive book. I also want to thank everyone from Union Square & Co. who contributed their expertise to help this book become what it is, including copyediting and illustrating.

I am endlessly grateful to my parents for always being supportive of my interests in the metaphysical and making sure Santa always got me at least some of the odd metaphysical books on my wish list. When I was in my teens, my mom got me my very first tarot deck and oracle deck. During her recent lengthy stays with us, my mother has been instrumental in the making of this book by helping take care of my kids so I could focus.

Special thanks to my dad for bringing me to my first metaphysical fairs, and for swapping stories of spirit communication with me, making it as normal as talking about the weather. And a big thanks to my stepmother Trine for being open and supportive of my work with zero judgement.

My kids deserve a big thanks as well, as they have been nothing but enthusiastic about this book, even when they didn't really believe I was writing an actual book. Both kids have said that when they grow up they want to be both a scientist (like their dad) and an animal communicator (like their mom), making for some baffled responses from their teachers. And though I am sure their interests and dreams will change, the thought has warmed my heart.

And to my amazing husband, Jon, I am deeply grateful. He supported me as I started my business years ago, and encouraged me to jump on the opportunity to write this book. Your support has meant the world.

Index

Note: Page references in *italics* indicate exercises.

INDEX

About the Author

THEA STROM is a medium, animal communicator, and mentor. She has been doing this work professionally since 2013, for clients all over the world, and collaborates regularly with animal rescues and other organizations. Thea is the creator of multiple online courses focused on developing animal communication, psychic, and mediumship abilities. One of her passions is to teach others how to develop their own abilities, connecting them to the spirit-world and animals all around them.

Thea was born in Oslo, Norway, but has been living in Oregon for the past 13 years. She lives with her husband, her two kids, two cats (Humphrey & Gilly), and a one-eyed guinea pig (Nutmeg). Aside from her spiritual work, she loves to spend time in nature, with animals, or on the couch with a good book.

Find out more about Thea and her work at her website and social media pages

www.theahealer.com

Instagram: @transcendingthea

Facebook: www.facebook.com/theahealer